Dear ?

Keep ?

dreams alive.

Best personal regards,
Dale Brown

GETTING OVER
THE FOUR
HURDLES
OF LIFE

GETTING OVER
THE FOUR
HURDLES
OF LIFE

Coach Dale Brown
With Dan Marin and Trent Angers

ISBN 10: 0-925417-72-6
ISBN 13: 978-0-925417-72-5

♦ Published by Acadian House Publishing, Lafayette,
  Louisiana (Edited by Trent Angers; designed and
  produced by Angelina Leger)

♦ Printed by Sheridan Books, Chelsea, Michigan

Introduction

On true success and peace of mind

By Shaquille O'Neal
Former LSU and NBA basketball player

There's a voice in each of us that says, "I've got to be somebody." Some of us start to hear this voice when we're kids; others hear it later in life.

It may be the voice of great ambition coming to life. Or it may be a more modest voice that says simply, "I want my life to count for something worthwhile."

For many, being somebody, being successful, means becoming rich and famous. But that's not really what true success is, as you will see in the early part of this book.

True success has a lot more to do with making a worthwhile contribution to society – whatever our lot in life, whatever our calling. It has to do with living decent lives, while doing our duty to the best of our ability, and with enjoying the peace of mind and sense of fulfillment that come with the territory.

This book is all about true success – and the hurdles we sometimes have to get over in order to achieve it. The author is the man who coached me while I played basketball for LSU, from 1989 to 1992, which were the best years of my life.

In the pages that follow, Coach Dale Brown writes about the four most common hurdles that people encounter in their efforts to lead successful and fulfilling lives.

He writes about the hurdle of handicaps, which affect so many people. And I'm not talking only about the physically handicapped, but about people who are handicapped by lack of ambition, low self-esteem, alcoholism, drug addiction, or extreme poverty that tends to keep them down.

He also writes about the hurdle of not knowing one's self, or lack of self-knowledge, which may be the trickiest and toughest problem for many of us. How are we ever going to have a happy and fulfilling life unless we know who we are? Tragically, many people don't figure this one out till most of their life is behind them.

Then there is the hurdle of past failures and/or fear of failure. Truth is, we all fail sometimes in life. I know I have. For one thing, I failed miserably at being even an average free throw shooter in the NBA and in college. I was so bad at it that some players on the opposing teams would foul me on purpose because it was a good bet I was going to miss the free throws. They even had a name for this strategy: "Hack-a-Shaq."

And finally, there is the hurdle called "I can't / You can't." This is the one that could have defeated me as a young man, before I got a good start in basketball. And I'm talking about high school basketball. I was a freshman, in the fall of 1985, and my coach cut me from the team, apparently thinking of me as a lost cause. He told me that wanting to play basketball and being able to play were two different things. He suggested I try out for another sport – possibly be a goalie in soccer – because I surely wasn't going to make it in basketball. I was too clumsy, too slow, my feet were too big.

Talk about crush a guy's self-esteem! What he said to me hurt me. I was wounded and felt insecure and uncertain of myself – all at the same time. I didn't want to believe him. I felt like I was destined to be a basketball player. I had the desire; I had the height. But when you're 13 years old you tend to believe what the coach tells you. You tend to take his words to heart. I was down but not completely out, though my self-confidence was deflated to the max.

Then I wrote to Coach Brown, whom I had met only a few months earlier. He seemed to think I was going to be a good player. He encouraged me and made me feel good about my potential the first time I met him. He wrote back and urged me to keep working at it, to do my very best, to think positive, and never give up.

Well, that's pretty much what he says when he gives his speech titled "The Four Hurdles of Life," and pretty much what he writes in this book. If we think positive, if we cultivate a positive vision of life, and not a negative one, we can get over the hurdles that block our path to success and happiness.

Now, getting over these hurdles is no cakewalk, as he points out. It takes commitment, hard work and stick-to-itiveness. But it can be done. I can vouch for the truth of what he has written and for the effectiveness of his formula for success and fulfillment in life. It has worked for me.

In fact, Coach Brown has taught me a lot of what I know about life and about basketball. He even tried to teach me to shoot free throws, but that didn't work out so well. Nobody's perfect!

But, seriously, it is a pleasure to introduce *Getting Over the 4 Hurdles of Life*, a book that is destined to change the lives of many.

Prologue

Preparing to take on life's adversities

Even before I began my career as a college basketball coach, the seeds of the hurdles-of-life metaphor were planted in me as a youth growing up on the windblown plains of North Dakota.

My positive vision of life began to take shape there, in the 1930s and '40s, against a contrasting background of poverty, embarrassment, and anger over injustices done to my mother. I was an insecure young man with a low sense of self-esteem – and for good reason.

I was born in 1935 during the Great Depression in Minot, North Dakota, population then about 17,000. Two days before I was born, my so-called father abandoned us – my mom; my sister Lorraine, age 12; my sister Eleanor, age 11; and me.

I would not see or speak with him until I was a senior in high school, when he appeared at my school one day when I was in Latin class and asked for me. I was excused from the classroom to meet him in the corridor. Our conversation, if it can be called that, lasted just a few seconds. Eight years later, when I was in the Army, I saw him again, in Enid, Oklahoma. This conversation, though slightly more extended, was to be our last.

It may be that his abandonment of us explains why I came to set so high a value on loyalty and persistence in the face of hardship.

My father's departure left my mother with only the $42.50 a month she received from the Welfare Department. Poverty hung over us like a dark, threatening cloud. Our very survival depended on my mother's making every penny count.

A girl from the farm with an eighth-grade education, the best she could do was domestic work – babysitting mostly. Her fragile health – a heart condition for which she took Digitalis; varicose veins; and other ailments as well – prevented her from undertaking heavy work. Nevertheless, despite hard circumstances, she remained all her life a gentle, soft-spoken soul, uncomplaining, and consequently too easily victimized and bullied by those around her who were inclined to do so.

One of these was the social worker from the Welfare Department, who paid us periodic visits to make sure my mother was not spending her money frivolously – which, of course, she never was.

It was as if poverty was a crime we had committed and the social worker was our parole officer to whom we were periodically accountable.

I vividly recall one day when the social worker checked up on us. I was home for my lunch, a bowl of soup. The social worker was speaking sternly to my mother.

"Do you realize, Mrs. Brown, that Ward County Welfare had to pay $13 last month for your Digitalis?"

I had no idea then what Digitalis was, but I could tell that the social worker's question made my mother exceedingly uncomfortable. The social worker wasn't done.

"And another thing: You're getting $42.50 a month. Go get your purse and let me see what you've got in it."

My mother went to the closet and got her purse and opened it. The social worker looked inside.

Even as a kid, 12 years old, I knew this was wrong, an injustice.

Indeed, injustice seemed to surround us. The landlady seized whatever opportunity arose to exercise her power over us – which usually took the form of threatening to evict us. For example, after school one day I came home and found my mother crying.

"Dale," she said, "you have to be careful out in the hall. That linoleum in the hall…"

She was referring to my habit of pretending that I was shooting baskets using a rolled up sock for a ball and the hot water pipes as my basket. The landlady had complained to her: I was scuffing up the linoleum.

"That little brat of yours," the landlady shouted, "you better keep him out of the hall, or you're going to have to find another place to stay."

Panic gripped my mother.

"What if she puts us out? Where will we go? What will we do?" she asked me.

Again, I was enraged by the lack of compassion, by the injustice of it. In my mind's eye I saw the landlady's face, framed by the little rectangular opening she had beside her door; she could open it to collect the rent, without leaving her quarters.

It upset and angered me that a gentle-hearted soul such as my own mother should be treated this way, that she should be subjected to the wrongful and undeserved exercise of the landlady's power to inflict pain and anxiety.

My anger overcame me. I beat on the landlady's door, and when her face appeared in the little rectangular opening, I shouted at her.

"You leave my mother alone!"

Then I turned on my heel and walked back down the hall toward our apartment, scuffing the linoleum as hard as I could.

The landlady never followed through on her threat to evict us. Maybe her power over us was not quite as great as my mother feared it to be.

Strangely, after that episode, the landlady and her husband befriended me. They even treated me to lunch and took me to the drive-in movies a few times. Occasionally, they would take me with them down to the Great Northern Railroad Depot, where together we would watch the trains take on big blocks of ice and other provisions.

Otherwise, however, harshness and difficulty seemed to rule even the smallest details of our daily existence. Mother, then in her mid-fifties and afflicted as she was with various health problems, would stand downstairs in the cold by the door, waiting for those for whom she babysat to pick her up. *Why couldn't these people come upstairs to our apartment?* I wondered. *So Mama could wait in the warmth of our apartment. Why couldn't these people show her respect and consideration?*

I couldn't understand the world's meanness and unfairness. It made no sense. I refused to accept it.

*   *   *

Our apartment was tiny, just one room for the four of us. It was directly over a hardware store, which was next door to a bar, a block west of Main Street and two blocks west of the Red Light District.

13

When my sisters were old enough and able to support themselves, they moved into another apartment on the same floor. Mama and I moved down the hall to an apartment with its own toilet and bathtub and a kitchen just a little bigger than the icebox. This was luxurious compared to our old apartment, where we had to share a bathroom and toilet with other renters. In this way, you might say, poverty introduced me to luxury.

But mostly, poverty introduced me to shame and guilt. Our poverty and the absence of a father embarrassed me and made me painfully self-conscious. I thought of my father as "my mother's husband," though I never heard her utter a bad word about him – or about anyone else for that matter. For years, whenever I filled out an application for a job, I wrote *deceased* in the space where it asked for my father's name.

In church, as I knelt at the altar rail to receive Holy Communion, I imagined that the parishioners behind me stared at the holes in the soles of my shoes and judged me accordingly. We didn't have money for shoe repair. As best I could I did my own cobbling. From popcorn boxes I saved from rare visits to the town movie house, I cut out cardboard in the shape of my shoes' soles and stuffed it inside my shoes. But I feared my makeshift repair efforts were visible all the same. I worried terribly about appearances.

Every day Mama took me to early Mass at St. Leo's Catholic Church, just a few blocks from where we lived. Cold, snow, wind didn't stop us. On a winter day I could see St. Leo's two red brick towers rising up through the snow as I trudged along with Mama. We walked past a drug store, a fire and police station, a light and gas company, clothing stores and several bars. Way down at the end of Main Street was the red brick Soo Line Depot, beyond which the hills rose gently to the north, toward Canada. This, daily, was my vision of the world from the center of Minot.

Sometimes, if it happened to be raining, I could feel the wetness seeping through the cardboard in my shoes. On such days I wished Mama would turn around and take us home. But she neither made nor accepted excuses. The dampness was simply one of life's obstacles to be overcome. Our destination was the church. Our purpose was to live according to its teachings, hard as that might be at times.

I never heard Mama complain. The word *can't* – as in "I can't walk in the rain with holes in my shoes," spoken from the warmth of my bed – didn't seem to be in her vocabulary. To my many pretended illnesses and other attempts to avoid going to church, my mother's response was always:

"Get up, son. We're going to Mass and Communion."

Even after the war, as far as we were concerned,

the Great Depression did not let up much in Minot, North Dakota. But poor as we were, Mama taught lessons about the dignity and self-worth of each human being, no matter his or her station in life. Her religious beliefs could be seen in the way she lived. She took the advice of Saint Francis of Assisi, who said in the 13th century, "Preach the gospel every day, and if necessary use words." There were lessons in her acts of refusal to complain about her circumstances or to ever speak negatively about the husband who abandoned her. She never asked for alimony. She never pursued a divorce. Her energies were concentrated instead on the task at hand: bringing us up properly.

Twice I remember watching her put on her winter coat and go down the flight of stairs from our apartment to the street to walk all the way back to the supermarket, once to return 25 cents and once to return 40 cents, because the clerk had mistakenly given her too much change.

She didn't need a PhD in theology to teach us honesty and integrity. For Mama, honesty and integrity were natural, intuitive knowledge.

Like many mothers, Mama could tell when I had something weighing on my mind. As a teenager, I had gotten in the habit of sitting out on our building's fire escape over the alley to be alone with my thoughts and to liberate myself from the confines of our one-room apartment. Out there my actual horizon was the brick wall of the building across the alley. But I spent my time there imagining and longing for a different life, a life beyond the hills that surrounded Minot.

One evening Mama asked me what I thought about out there all alone on the fire escape. I told her I imagined traveling to exotic places like Paris, Egypt, the Orient. I told her I saw myself climbing mountains, mountains beyond mountains, the Matterhorn. And on top of all this, I said, I wanted to learn as much as I could; I was curious about everything, driven to know.

Mama heard me out then hesitated a moment, as if deciding something.

"You know, son, I'm going to tell you something," she said.

I didn't know then that the story she was about to tell me of her own encounter with shame and her desire to escape the poverty and constraints of her situation in life would reach so far and resonate so broadly and long in *my* life. What she said introduced me to two of the most essential and difficult of life's challenges: knowing and respecting yourself.

"You know, when these big shots come to pick me up to go babysit, I'm so embarrassed. There's no husband in our house. We live in this little one-room apartment. We're on welfare. I've just got an eighth-grade education. I worry about my image when these people come to pick me up. So I look up big words in the dictionary and then all the way to their house I inject these words into the conversation to impress them."

She paused so I could take that in.

"That's called making an image," she continued, inclining a little toward me for gentle emphasis. "Out there on the fire escape it's just you and God. God knows who you are. That's your true character. Son, if you spend too much time polishing your image, you'll eventually tarnish your character, and you'll be an unhappy man."

Mama realized that her pretending to be someone she was not – designed as it was to cover her feelings of inferiority – merely intensified her shame. Shame is internal and can't be hidden from oneself. The truth is that in God's eyes she was not inferior at all, and to regard herself as inferior was to fail to recognize her true self and to devalue His creation.

But the lessons she was trying to teach me were clear: Don't pretend to be someone you're not; don't let other people tell you who you are; and don't try to escape your true self, because this will only end in unhappiness. For her, strength lay in the humble acceptance of herself as a creation of God.

Most importantly, she taught me that my own human dignity and self-worth were real and could lift me above the confines of the little world in which we lived. I didn't have to travel, or climb the Matterhorn, or have a fancy education to achieve human dignity and self-worth. These traits are God-given. I merely had to be myself.

The little talks Mama and I had filled our small apartment with good spirit and thereby greatly enlarged it. It was these talks – coupled with lessons I learned about compassion and discipline while attending Catholic school for 12 years – that fortified me against the adversities and challenges that would come my way as I ventured out into the world beyond Minot, North Dakota.

Acknowledgements

Quite a few people contributed to making this book the best it could be, and I offer my sincere gratitude to them all.

Those who reviewed the galleys for logic, structure, grammar and the like: Darlene Smith, Jim Talbot, Jeffrey Marx, John Boudreaux and Don Yaeger.

Three special people who helped us get certain critical facts straight: Jackie Maravich McLachlan, widow of Pete Maravich; Glenda Anderson Leonard, widow of Paul Anderson; and Kent Lowe of the LSU Sports Information Department.

The staff of Acadian House Publishing: Trent Angers, Editor & Publisher; Angelina Leger, Art Director; and proofreaders/fact-checkers Jimmy Connell, Claire Gamble and Rebecca Padgett. Thanks also to Kaz Baczinskas for his work on the Bill W. story, which starts on page 110.

My assistant, Linda Pourciau, and Assistant to the Publisher, Anna Elledge, who contributed in countless ways to help this project move forward as smoothly as possible.

– D.B.

This book is dedicated to three women who have helped me to become exactly who I am:

My dear mother, Agnes, who was the most honest human being I have ever known and who provided for me under very difficult circumstances

My loyal wife, Vonnie, a great teacher, an independent spirit, always a steady source of common sense

My daughter, Robyn, so special and caring, an absolute blessing, who has brought so much joy into my life.

Table of Contents

GETTING OVER
THE FOUR
HURDLES
OF LIFE

Chapter 1

Letters to Shaq

In the summer of 1993, I wrote to Shaquille O'Neal congratulating him on completing his first successful professional basketball season. He had been voted the NBA 1993 Rookie of the Year.

"Dear Shaquille," I began. "Congratulations on a great rookie year in the NBA. I am so proud of you and especially of the manner in which you conducted yourself."

Shaquille's impact on the game of basketball was immediate and significant, both at the college level and in the pros. He was the NBA's number one draft pick at the end of his junior year at LSU. While attending LSU he had averaged 22 points and 13 rebounds a game. Then he helped his pro team, the

Orlando Magic, win 20 more games than they had won the previous season. Both on and off the court, he had displayed class and dignity.

In my letter to Shaq, I recalled our first meeting in the mountains of West Germany back in 1985. I had met him at the U.S. military base at Wildflecken, near the East-West German border where, on behalf of the United States Army, I was speaking to the soldiers about leadership and teamwork. It was my last stop before heading home from a series of talks to our troops who were massed near the East German border, conducting military maneuvers as a means of discouraging communist aggression. In addition to my regular talk, I had agreed to give a basketball clinic for the soldiers at Wildflecken. I was behind the podium packing up when someone gently tapped my shoulder.

"Excuse me, Coach Brown?"

The guy who wanted to talk with me was friendly and very tall. He looked to be 6-foot-9 and 250 pounds. His shoulders were broad, his feet were huge. Dressed neatly in khakis and a sport shirt, his demeanor was polite and respectful.

"Coach," he said, "I plan to go out for the team. But big as I am, I can't dunk the ball; when I run up and down the court I tire quickly in my lower extremities. Can you show me some exercises to help me?"

"Sure can, soldier," I said. "What's your name?"

"Shaquille O'Neal."

I came around from behind the podium and showed him a couple of exercises to strengthen his legs and improve his jumping ability.

"When I get back to Baton Rouge, I'll send you our weight-training program," I told him. "By the way, how long have you been in the service, soldier?"

He grinned broadly, then leaned down and sort of shielded his mouth with the back of his huge hand, then whispered.

"Coach, I'm not in the service. I'm only 13 years old," he said, explaining that he was in Germany because his father was a career sergeant in the army.

"Just 13, huh?" I said as I looked up at him with some degree of amazement.

I then asked if his father was around.

He said his dad, Sgt. Philip Harrison, was in the sauna.

"I'd like to meet him," I said.

Shaquille was determined to be a basketball player. He was a freshman at the high school in the small town of Fulda, some 12 miles northwest of the Wild-flecken army base. He intended to try out for the team. So many people assumed he was a basketball player – probably because of his size – that he felt an obligation, a calling, to be on the team. He believed basketball was his destiny, which he had to fulfill no matter what obstacles, what hurdles, stood in his way.

After visiting with Shaquille for a little while, he took me to meet his dad. Sgt. Harrison took the business card I handed him, held it up to the light, and looked at it warily, almost with disdain. He was a big man and had been a talented college basketball player himself. He was okay with basketball as long as it didn't interfere with Shaquille's getting a solid education. Provided I understood that, Sgt. Harrison said, we would stay in touch.

I immediately liked Sgt. Harrison's directness about his priorities. We shook hands. I said I hoped Shaquille would let me know how he was doing, on as well as off the basketball court.

I got back to Baton Rouge and right away sent Shaquille a copy of our weight-training program, complete with instructions and diagrams.

Six weeks later, as I was going down the hall on my way to practice, my secretary came running after me.

"Coach, I think you'll want this," she said.

She handed me a letter. It was from Shaquille.

"Coach, I did everything you told me to do. The coach cut me from the team. He told me I'm too clumsy, I'm too slow, my feet are too big. He told me I could never play basketball; I should try out for goalie on the soccer team. Coach, what should I do?"

I put Shaquille's letter in my pocket. But all through practice I was distracted. What profound thing could I possibly say to this young man that would help him? After practice I went to my office, sat down at my desk, and started writing.

"Dear Shaquille, I'm sorry about what happened

with the basketball team. But I sincerely believe that if you try to do your very best, if you never give up, God will take care of the rest."

Well, apparently Shaquille rejected that high school coach's assessment of him, because four years later he was at LSU as a college freshman. And he made the starting five.

Perseverance in the face of discouragement, the will to stay positive and to confront and overcome obstacles, and the courage to reject the verdict of those who say "You can't" – I like that in a person.

I liked Shaquille from our first meeting. His broad, contagious smile signaled a positive disposition and a generous nature. Just from the little I knew about him then, I couldn't accept his high school basketball coach's verdict. Shaquille looked like a basketball player to me. His determination and perseverance piqued my interest. Where the high school coach apparently saw only obstacles – too clumsy, too slow, feet too big – I saw a young man with great possibilities.

In his NBA rookie year Shaquille, at age 21, reached a level of professional athletic achievement attained by very few players in an entire career. I felt proud of him and I also felt called – as his college coach and mentor – to alert him to the pressures and dangers of the world, including agents of corrosion and distortion who make a living preying upon such high achievers as him.

"Being constantly in the spotlight," I wrote, "you must be alert to all the pressures it brings."

My letter to Shaquille was about more than basketball skills and achievements. I knew the lives of athletes are fraught with distractions. "The succession of time and events," as the Genevan philosopher Jean-Jacques Rousseau tells us, "can disfigure the human soul... (and change) its appearance to the point where it is almost impossible to recognize." Now, if you conduct a search on your computer for Shaquille O'Neal, you'll find hundreds of thousands of entries. All of this recognition could, if he let it, add up to a lot of distraction and disfigurement of his soul.

"Stay away from all distractions," I wrote, "because concentration is imperative for ultimate success."

I told him to be on the lookout for "parasites who, for selfish motives, want you to be their friend." I urged him to make his mark on the world, not only as a basketball player but as a human being. I urged him to "leave a legacy beyond trophies and statistics," to be his brother's keeper, and to "lift your brother up when he has fallen." Shaquille had about him a natural grace and dignity, clearly discernable in the way he spoke and moved, both on and off the court.

To get a true picture of Shaquille O'Neal, his full *human* stature, imagine him, now 7-foot-1, 345 pounds, 15-time NBA All Star, named as "one of the 50 greatest players in the NBA." He is hunched behind the steering wheel of his SUV. He peers through the dark New Orleans streets after Hurricane Katrina as he follows the 18-wheeler he has hired for the relief effort. Ahead, on either side of the headlights' broad beams, are piles of wreckage and debris of homes and lives. Not many people know about this charitable act, not even those who benefited from it, because Shaquille did it quietly, without calling attention to himself. Shaquille is one of the most genuine and benevolent athletes I have ever met, loaded not only with talent but with heart and goodness toward others.

So, I begin this book about the four hurdles of life with Shaquille O'Neal's story because in his progress and growth as a human being I see the triumph of a positive vision of life over life's obstacles.

Faced with discouragement, told that he couldn't be a basketball player, he told himself I *will* be a basketball player. Told that his size, clumsiness, lack of quickness, and huge feet were *dis*advantages, he set about turning them into *ad*vantages. He would build up his strength.

Cut from his high school team his freshman year, he refused to accept this setback as the last word on his possibilities. Despite those who tried to tell him who he was or wasn't, he stuck to his own vision of himself.

At the LSU Summer Basketball Camp in 1995, Shaquille inspired the participants in a brief motivational address:

"People always used to tell me when I was young, 'You're not going to be anything.' But I never gave up. If you work hard, stay out of trouble, and follow your dreams, you can be anyone you want. I promise you."

It was good advice, not only for aspiring young athletes but for anyone at any age who sincerely wants to make a positive and meaningful contribution to the world in which we live.

Chapter 2

In search of a positive vision of life

s a college basketball coach and even after retiring from coaching, I've made it a practice to promote a positive vision of life because I believe it is essential to success and peace of mind.

This positive vision is in itself a kind of achievement – something good for its own sake – but it is also instrumental in the achievement of other important goals in life.

Positive thinking gives us strength and courage; it releases energy and power in us we may not have known we had. It can help lift us over most any obstacle, any hurdle, life puts in our path.

I've seen it work. I'm writing from my own experience, first as a young boy who grew up in poverty in a household with no father during the Great Depression in Minot, North Dakota; then as a life-long coach and mentor of young athletes. I've seen firsthand what this positive vision can do for those who choose it.

Surely, I don't deny life's difficulties and obstacles, its hurdles, but I lean strongly toward an optimistic view of human possibilities.

And I'm certainly not alone in this point of view. Many noted writers and speakers have embraced it as absolutely essential to a life of happiness and fulfillment. For instance, Dr. Robert Schuller, founder of the Crystal Cathedral in Garden Grove, California, authored a book titled *Possibility Thinking*, wherein he suggested many possible ways by which – taking a positive-minded approach – we can solve problems of various kinds. During the recession of the early 1980s he wrote another popular book – *Tough Times Never Last, But Tough People Do* – encouraging his readers to be strong, to toughen up, and to approach problems with courage, optimism and imagination.

The foremost advocate of positive-mindedness was Dr. Norman Vincent Peale, author of *The Power of Positive Thinking*. For decades, beginning in the 1930s, he lifted people's spirits and emboldened readers by the tens of thousands. One of his most famous passages, one that continues to bolster my spirits every time I read it, goes like this:

> So if you feel that you are defeated and have lost
> confidence in your ability to win, sit down, take a
> piece of paper and make a list, not of the factors that
> are against you, but of those that are for you. If you or
> I think constantly of the forces that seem to be against
> us, they will assume a formidable strength they do not
> possess. But if you mentally visualize and affirm and
> reaffirm your assets, you will rise out of any difficulty.
> Your inner powers will reassert themselves and, with
> the help of God, lift you to victory.

The counting of one's blessings is certainly a key component of the positive approach to life which I advocate. All of us would do well to slow down and be still and take stock of how blessed we truly are.

As a coach and mentor of young men, I always felt it was my job, my vocation, to uplift them, to speak positively and optimistically, to bring forward a strong, positive vision of life. And I can tell you that this vision is infectious. It spreads. It energizes. I've seen it with my own eyes.

And, as a result, things get accomplished that few people thought would be accomplished.

I brought this vision with me when I first went to Louisiana State University, where traditionally basketball played second fiddle to football. Louisiana had been a football state for a long time. In football, with Paul Dietzel as head coach, 14 years before I got there, LSU had been collegiate national football champions. The football team had a tradition of winning.

In 1972, the year I arrived, local sports writer Dan Hardesty picked the LSU basketball team to finish last in the SEC. He hinted it would be a greater miracle than Lazarus rising from the dead if LSU won more than two games. Things hadn't been going well for a long time. LSU had had four winning seasons in the previous 18. I inherited a team thought to have very little talent.

One of its bright spots had been Pete Maravich, whose father, Coach Press Maravich, I was hired to replace. Pete recently had moved on to phenomenal success in the NBA.

So, in the wake of all this, when I came on like gangbusters at LSU with my can-win attitude and positive vision of life, there were people who said I was being unrealistic, overly optimistic. Some, I'm sure, regarded me as being out of touch with reality.

The critics had their say. But our team's record spoke louder, giving credence to the power of a positive vision. From 1972 through 1997, LSU won 448 games, 238 in the SEC. During that stretch, our team had the most wins by an LSU team in a season, 31; our team had the most consecutive wins in a season, 26; most consecutive national tournament appearances by an SEC team, 15; and so on.

And here's the thing: We achieved what we achieved with teams of very uneven talent – some years little talent, some years terrific talent, some years mediocre talent.

My first year, the one in which we were picked to win only two games and finish in the SEC cellar, we beat the nation's third-ranked team and eventual NCAA Championship runner-up, Memphis State, 94-81. That season we won 14 games and finished in the SEC's top five. Talent is important, but it's not the only thing that's important.

I don't recite these achievements to boast but to demonstrate that as much as anything else it was attitude and philosophy that shaped and anchored our team.

Plain and simple, our team did well not only because of their talent and hard work but also because of their positive vision. They believed they could win; they believed they *would* win. And this belief brought out the very best in them.

*   *   *

A positive vision of life can be tough to come by in our world today, flooded as we are daily with bad news and adversity.

You see it the moment you spread your morning paper on the kitchen table and read the headlines. You get the same effect by turning on the TV news. A rising tide of bad news and adversity threatens to overwhelm us. Too much of it can result in a negative vision of life – which appears to have become the norm of our society.

Our proliferating channels of communication

keep us in touch constantly with not only the local bad news but with tragic events affecting people all over the world. From our newspapers, car radios, TVs, the Internet, cell phones, iPhones and smart phones there pours a flood of bad tidings: murder, rape, pedophilia, swindles and scandals, economic decline, high unemployment numbers, bankruptcies, plant closures, foreclosures, war, genocides, starvation, terrorism, sleazy politicians, and global climate change. We are swept up in a Noah's flood of the depressing details of Bernie Madoff's Ponzi scheme, Enron's collapse and the tragedy of Somalia's forlorn orphan children.

Think also about how darkness and adversity seep into our private lives: alcoholism, drug addiction, domestic violence, divorce, abandonment. It's an epidemic, a plague of afflictions rivaling those suffered by Egypt in the days of Moses.

All these, publicly dramatized by the public lives of certain celebrities, nevertheless confirm our commonality. We are in touch. We are bonded. Everywhere we meet people who have a son, a daughter, a relative, or a friend who has relapsed and is back in rehab.

We sympathize. We identify. The adversity we suffer becomes a social bond, connecting us to others.

The accumulation of connections has added three new verbs to our common vocabulary: We now "blog" and "text" and "tweet." Too many of us willingly participate – personally and publicly – in this negativity. It's a ritual that is played out daily.

Try this experiment. Imagine walking into a room full of your fellow workers and complaining loudly about the terrible working conditions, the lousy pay, the oppressive supervisor, the idiotic company policies, whatever there is about which you might complain. Chances are you'll get nods of agreement. They know what you're talking about.

Now, imagine walking into the same room full of the same fellow workers and talking about your pleasure in your work and job satisfaction, appreciation of the working conditions and pay, admiration for your boss, support for the company policies.

What's the reaction going to be? Silence most likely. Or someone may exclaim, "What a Pollyanna attitude!" No shared feelings here. It's hard to imagine otherwise. Why? Because complaining is our daily custom. It's the norm; we are mired in negativity.

But that's not the end of it.

Probably the worst of it is that we let our failures define us. We let them tell us who we are. Instead of learning how to succeed from our failed efforts, we start to believe that we can't succeed. Or we learn to excuse our failures by citing our shortcomings, our handicaps.

The lesson learned and reinforced over and over is the same: "I can't do this, or I can't do that. My failures are not my fault; how can I help but be unhappy? I am who I am."

With this attitude, with this false view of who we are, we feel helpless, which only compounds our sense of failure. Our dignity and integrity are thus eroded.

So, what some of us do is we sink into to self-deception, and in company we pretend to be somebody we're not. We fake happiness. We tend to measure our success with material wealth, but since we know deep down that we're faking it, we remain acutely unhappy, unable to placate ourselves with the outward signs of success. We are rich in things and maybe even famous, but nevertheless miserably unfulfilled.

Down in the dim cave of pretense, there is too little light to see who we truly are. Our reality is comprised of shadows of reality. And with only this dim shadowy knowledge of who we are, how can we possibly live a good life? How can we approach the true peace of mind that we deeply desire? We keep searching.

All of us want to be lifted up. We want to get out of this sea of negativity, uncertainty and self-deception. We want to come out into the light. We have this natural craving – like a physical hunger in the pit of our stomach – for a positive and meaningful vision of life. I am writing this book to respond to that hunger.

Chapter 3

Genesis of 'The 4 Hurdles' metaphor

he metaphor of the four hurldes of life came to me in the mid-1970s during a meeting with Ron Abernathy, one of my assistant coaches.

As far as Southeastern Conference basketball was concerned, we were both new kids on the block. Right away I felt a kinship with Ron. He had started at the bottom of the ladder, in high school coaching, as I had, and worked his way up. Ron had played basketball at Morehead State University in Kentucky and then started coaching in Louisville.

He was about the most optimistic, uplifting person you'd ever want to know. Very seldom did I hear Ron say anything negative about anybody. He was naturally inclined to think the best about everyone.

He was eager to do things the right way, to play by the rules. He was an idealist, which is another reason I felt a kinship with him.

But one day I found Ron uncharacteristically agitated and dejected, not his usual upbeat self. We had been talking about recruiting. Ron was telling me how frustrating it was, how you go out and try to get close to these guys you are recruiting. You play by the rules. And then a recruiter from another school comes along and tells the guy he can fix a grade to get him in college, or he makes him a whole litany of other improper if not illegal offers. Or he promises something else: "You'll be a starter your freshman year."

"This is really frustrating. It angers me," Ron said. "How can we play fair and succeed under such conditions?"

"Ron, I know exactly what you're talking about. Sometimes you feel you're about to explode, it's so unfair. If you play by the rules, success seems just out of reach. There are too many things in the way, obstacles you have to go over," I said.

And then, speaking from my own experience, remembering the poverty and hardship of my childhood growing up in North Dakota, I said:

"Listen, life's a series. You get knocked down and beaten up, but then you get up again. That's how it is. It's a series of... hurdles. You've got to get over each one and go on to the next one. If you dwell on the one you just stumbled on, you won't get over the one in front of you. And in life you don't win every race."

Suddenly, *hurdles* seemed a simple and convenient way to say it, to draw a picture of the difficulties in life that we all must face. I didn't have the whole idea yet, merely a preliminary sketch. At that moment, I was just trying to draw a mental picture that would make sense of the feeling of frustration Ron and I shared in recruiting.

I could see it. You're trying to get from the starting blocks down the track, over the hurdles placed at regular intervals, to the finish line. Let's call getting to the finish line in your best time *success*. Beyond the finish line, at least for the moment, you'll experience a relaxing of muscles and peace of mind. But for now, between you and this momentary feeling of release, there are hurdles to get over.

When you're new at it, as Ron and I were – just starting out at LSU, trying to build the basketball program – you will sometimes stumble and fall, but you've got to get up and keep running. You do the best you can and when you cross the line you know you gave it your best shot. Then comes that period of relaxation and peace of mind.

That's the simple picture I wanted to draw for Ron to reassure him, though, of course, we both knew that in the end success and peace of mind don't come as simply or easily or as regularly as my sketch made it seem. For one thing, life's hurdles are not placed at regular intervals on a nice all-weather track.

That spontaneous sketch, that epiphany, was a kind of catalyst, a spark. It started me thinking; it raised lots of questions. I asked myself, *Okay, what do we really mean by success? What constitutes true success?*

What gets between us and achieving this true success? Life's hurdles? Okay, what are life's hurdles?

How do we learn to get over them without stumbling? Or if we do stumble, as all of us are bound to do sometimes, how do we get back up?

No matter what we are trying to do, there are going to be failures, so what's the role of failure in a successful life?

What do we really have to do to be successful?

I ran track in high school and college, the quarter mile, but not the hurdles. Nevertheless, I respected and admired the good hurdlers I saw at the track meets. It took tremendous discipline and confidence to slip over each hurdle so easily and efficiently, with no discernable break in stride. Some hurdlers were so precise it seemed they could knock a penny off the top of a hurdle with the heel of their shoe without touching the hurdle itself.

However, I knew that even a very good athlete might occasionally hit a hurdle and stumble or even fall. I saw it a couple of times. But the good hurdlers got up and went on, and the next week's practice restored their confidence. They built future success on past failures by learning from their failures.

And so it is with the hurdles of life: No one succeeds without stumbling.

*   *   *

That conversation with Ron back in 1976 launched me on a search. I rolled these questions over in my mind, this way and that. I started making notes on legal pads.

One of the most interesting discoveries came to me courtesy of a friend and neighbor, Jeffrey Marx, who called me one day to share something he had just learned. A journalist, Jeffrey had been doing research at the Library of Congress in Washington, D.C., and had come across the first Webster's dictionary, published in 1806. He and I were both intrigued by what the old book offered as the definition of success.

It listed the attributes of the successful person as "prosperous," "fortunate," "happy," and "kind." The most recent edition of Webster's, however, says success means "attainment of wealth, favor, and eminence."

Being successful had thus become tantamount to creating the illusion of success. Being successful had become *appearing* to be successful.

The world bombards us with the images of this material success. It seems that in current usage happiness and kindness have dropped out of the picture.

I read stacks of books about positive thinking,

about people who maintained a positive vision of life and succeeded – like Napoleon Hill, who wrote *Think and Grow Rich*, Norman Vincent Peale, who wrote *The Power of Positive Thinking*, and Olympian Bob Richards, who wrote *The Heart of a Champion*. I made lists of people who had gotten over life's hurdles.

The hurdles metaphor had started me thinking, but intuition, reinforced by experience, told me that life was more complicated than most of the representations of it in books. The truth is that life is chock-full of adversity. It's inevitable, and we never know when we'll have to deal with it.

In such a world, how could the optimism and idealism of a Ron Abernathy prosper and end in success? How could Ron sustain his positive vision of life? How could I sustain mine? So, I immersed myself in the pursuit of answers to questions such as these.

Chapter 4

The 4 Hurdles of Life

ight after my conversation with Coach Ron Abernathy about life's hurdles, I started making notes and collecting stories about people like Walt Disney, Elvis Presley, Paul Anderson and Albert Einstein.

Stories attesting to the importance of a positive vision of life came to me from all directions. I wrote down lots of notes about how people overcame the obstacles that blocked their way to a better life. I gathered articles and read books that inspired me, a few that moved me nearly to tears. There were stories about some of the greatest athletes, the most prolific writers, the most talented entertainers, the most brilliant minds – all of them noble men and women of character, all of them refusing to be defeated by adversity.

As I studied the lives of these heroic people, a certain pattern emerged. The difficulties they had to deal with seemed to cluster around four themes, four particular hurdles that were in the way of their success and happiness:

1. **"I can't"** and **"You can't"** do this or that.

2. **Past failures** and/or **fear of failure** – obstacles that can paralyze us into inaction, and stop us dead in our tracks.

3. **Handicaps** – whether physical, psychological, financial or career-based.

4. **Lack of self-knowledge** – for many, the most difficult hurdle to get over.

The way I see it is that from the day we are born, we are starting down a track of hurdles we have to get over. But unlike the tracks I ran on in high school and college, life's track extends for a lifetime.

One thing about these hurdles is that *you* have to go over them. Nobody can do that for you. *You* have to commit to do your very best every day.

If I've said it once, I've said it a thousand times: Every day, do your best, don't give up, and God will do the rest. If you're seriously committed, if you're determined, you can get over the hurdles of life. And once you get over them you can truly enjoy success and happiness.

When I give a talk about the four hurdles of life, I ask the group sponsoring my talk to have four chairs, each representing one of the hurdles, placed on the apron of the stage in front of and a little to the side of the speaker's podium. These are my props. However, although they will be useful – helping my audience to visualize the hurdles as I explain and illustrate each in its turn – I know the hurdles are not as separable as the image created by the props.

Life, as we all know, turns out to be not so neatly arranged and orderly; it's messier. As I have said, life's hurdles won't necessarily occur at regular intervals on a nice all-weather Tartan track. In the real world, offstage, the ground is not so level, nor the intervals so regular; and the hurdles often come in bunches.

And the older I get, the more life's hurdles remind me of a steeplechase course, liberally sprinkled with muddy puddles, so that at the race's end the runners, as often as not, turn up bespattered with mud. That's more the way life is. There's a lot of mud and messiness along the way – all the more reason for us to develop and embrace a positive vision of life to strengthen us to deal with life's inevitable difficulties.

*   *   *

Sometime in the spring of 2010, a friend sent me a link to an inspiring video of the 2009 V Foundation Awards program.

The foundation, established to provide funds for cancer research, was founded by ESPN and North Carolina State basketball coach Jimmy Valvano in

1993. A year earlier, Jimmy V, as he was called, had been diagnosed with metastatic bone cancer. He remained positive and fought valiantly against the cancer but finally succumbed to it.

But tonight, for the 2009 awards presentation, another courageous basketball coach was being honored: Don Meyer, head coach of the Northern State University team, located in Aberdeen, South Dakota.

The emcee began the ceremony by observing that unlike some names in the basketball coaching world, the name Don Meyer was not widely known. Then the lights dimmed and Don's career began to play out on the auditorium's huge screen – Don coaching, talking with players, signaling instructions from the sideline.

Don Meyer, the video's narrator informed the audience, had been a "mentor and coach to all who had known him for 38 seasons." He had been on the verge of winning more games than any men's college basketball coach in history.

But on September 5, 2008, Don was badly injured in a head-on collision with an 18-wheeler. Don was driving a van, leading a caravan of vehicles bringing his players home from a practice game. It was late at night and Don was tired and dozed off at the wheel. He was the only one seriously injured. The players, who had learned from Don to react calmly and reasonably in a crisis – "do the next necessary thing," he had preached – called 911 for help.

Don's ribs were crushed, his chest cavity flooded with blood; his spleen and diaphragm destroyed; his left leg mangled.

And there was more bad news. During surgery following the accident, doctors discovered cancer in Don's liver and intestine.

After the surgery, his daughter Brittany tells us, the tube down his throat prevented him from talking, and he couldn't move except to wiggle his right hand.

"So we put a pen in his hand, and he wrote on a piece of paper, 'How long before I can coach?'"

Fourteen days later, doctors amputated his left leg below the knee.

After 55 days in the hospital, Don left in a wheelchair and was at work at 4:45 the next morning. He did not miss a single game the entire season. On January 10, 2009, his team presented him with his 903rd win, setting a collegiate coaching record, which has since been extended to 923. Don's achievement, the video's narrator told the audience, was "powered by faith, tenacity and a love of coaching."

Now, to a standing ovation, Don walked, with the aid of a walker, onto the stage and stood straight as a soldier at the podium. Behind him he appeared on the screen larger than life. He spoke with a strong, firm voice, but with humility and humor.

"I'm just a small-college coach from Northern State University in Aberdeen, South Dakota," he said, straight-faced. "That means that when I leave the motel tomorrow morning at 4:15 I'll take all the soap, shampoo and even..." – and here he paused to allow the applause and laughter to subside, then went on as straight-faced as before – "and even the shower cap."

A wave of laughter rippled through the audience. Don continued:

"It means I know how to make a 17-hour drive to spend two hours with a recruit and his family and then get back in the car and drive 17 hours back."

If he hadn't coached small-college basketball for nearly four decades, he told the audience, he probably wouldn't have developed the toughness it took to "successfully negotiate the past ten months."

He said he had had the good fortune of talking with legendary coach John Wooden the day before. Some years earlier, Coach Wooden had passed along to Don a card printed with guidance his father had given him upon grade school graduation. One of the elder Wooden's favorite pieces of advice was, "Don't whine, don't complain, and don't make excuses." This statement, Don said, came to mind every time he went to work out at rehab and glanced around the room at the others there – "and saw how much tougher they had it than I did."

Still perfectly straight-faced, he observed that it was unfortunate that "f-words" were used so much in our society and that "at Northern, we frequently use them in our basketball program." Then, lest the audience misunderstand, he explained:

"The 'f-words' we use are *faith, family and friends.*"

"*Faith* in God – faith that God had a reason for sparing my life at this time, so I try to serve others for a few more years. *Family* – such as my wife Carmen and our children, Jerry, Brooke and Brittany, who have given me constant concern, care and prayer. I would not be here tonight if my wife of 42 years had not devoted her entire time to bringing me back from where I was. *Friends* – including all the players and coaches from all over the country who have sent letters and e-mails and have encouraged me and visited me and sat up with me all night long while my wife got some rest so she could get up the next day and make the big decisions."

Just before he closed, Don offered a lesson.

"I have learned from this odyssey that peace is not the absence of trouble, trial and torment, but calm in the midst of them," he said.

His lesson spoke directly to me about the nature of the four hurdles of life – and about the self-control and discipline it must have taken for him to transcend the life-threatening injuries that might have defeated a lesser man.

For Don Meyer, it seemed that most of life's major hurdles had come in a bunch. Doctors had given him little chance of returning to coaching. It appeared at the time that the record 903rd victory would be out of reach. But in a wheelchair and despite the exhausting ordeal of chemotherapy treatments, he did not miss a game that season – and he was the coach on the bench when his team achieved the record-breaking win.

Chapter 5

The First Hurdle:
'I can't / You can't'

The first hurdle of life is called "I can't" or, what's just as bad or even worse, others telling you that "You can't."

Unfortunately, we often receive these discouraging messages from the very people who should be encouraging us – parents and other family members, spouses, friends, bosses and "significant others" of every kind.

For a few reasons, I am fully confident we can overcome the hurdles of life, including this one. For one thing, I believe most of us only scratch the surface of our potential greatness. We have billions of brain cells, 90 percent of which may never be used. We have awesome problem-solving potential by which we can think our way out of most any problem – when we are committed to doing so. And this faculty is not the exclusive domain of the highly educated. It is common to human beings in general – universal, natural, and God-given.

Of course, it's true that everyone has negative thoughts. We all hoard up reasons why "I can't" achieve this or that. We have a wide range of excuses, some of which are, of course, unavoidable conditions: lack of financial resources, insufficient education, shortage of opportunity, not knowing "the right people" to get this job or to achieve that goal.

But if we blame our lack of success or our unhappiness on others we won't be able to bring about the change of heart necessary to turn things around. By placing the blame on others, we abdicate control of our present and our future. Blaming others disempowers us from solving our problems; taking responsibility for our actions and their outcomes does the opposite: It empowers us.

When an "expert" tells you why you can't do what you want to do, that's a strong negative message that may not be easily overcome, a high hurdle that you'll have to get over somehow.

The solution, in part, is to replace negative thoughts and messages with positive ones – and to associate with positive-minded people, especially those who have your best interests at heart. It also helps a lot to read books and listen to CDs that feed your mind with material that engenders a positive mental attitude, that builds self-esteem, and that enlivens the mind and spirit.

Toward this end, I've gathered numerous stories of prominent people who overcame the hurdle of "I can't / You can't" to achieve remarkable success. For example:

• Elvis Presley, the King of Rock 'n' Roll, was told he would never make it as a singer, didn't have the voice.

• Albert Einstein, perhaps the most brilliant scientific mind in history, was branded "the dopey one" early in life and was not expected to contribute much to society.

• Walt Disney, the builder of an American entertainment empire, went bankrupt at age 21 while trying to make a living as a cartoon animator.

• Rudy Ruettiger, one of only two Notre Dame football players ever to be carried off the field by fellow players, was told many times that he was too small and too slow to play college football.

Each of these people was told in one way or another, "You can't." Each, early in life, faced a wall of discouragement. Each, whatever self-doubts he may have wrestled with, overcame seemingly insurmountable obstacles to achieve wide recognition and success.

They heard destiny calling. They refused to listen to the voices of experience and authority whose mantra was so negative and discouraging: "You're not college material," "You're too small to play football," "You've got to know the right people," "No way," "No-can-do," "Dream on!"

*   *   *

Elvis Presley:
'Never going to make it as a singer'

Elvis Presley was born in a shotgun house built by his father in Tupelo, Mississippi, in the middle of the Great Depression. An identical twin brother, delivered 35 minutes ahead of him, was stillborn, so Elvis was an only child.

Growing up, he loved the Gospel singers at the Assembly of God church his family attended. His interest in music grew as he entered grade school, and he got his first guitar for his tenth birthday. In the sixth grade Elvis, a loner, took his guitar to school, where he played it and sang at lunchtime. He was referred to by a classmate as the "trashy kid who played hillbilly music."

His family moved to Memphis, and Elvis devoted himself to his guitar and his music. But in the eighth grade he made just a C in music, lacking "aptitude for singing," according to his teacher. The next day he brought his guitar to school and sang "Keep Them Icy Fingers Off Me," to show what he could do. But his teacher remained unimpressed, saying she didn't "appreciate his kind of singing."

By the time he was a junior in high school, he was hanging around on Beale Street, soaking up the blues scene. Elvis never had any formal music training and couldn't read music; he studied and played by ear.

In 1953 Elvis walked into Sun Records, where an aspiring musician could pay for a few minutes of studio time. He said he wanted to make a record as a gift for his mother. A biographer claims he chose Sun Records hoping to be discovered. In any event, he recorded "My Happiness" and "That's When Your Heartaches Begin."

He made a second recording the next year: "I'll Never Stand in Your Way" and "It Wouldn't Be the Same Without You." But nothing came of any of these recordings.

Then he failed an audition with the Songfellows vocal quartet. Elvis told his father, "They told me I couldn't sing." Songfellow Jim Hamill attributed the failure to Elvis's lacking an ear for harmony.

So, Elvis took a job as a truck driver.

Elvis' friend, Ronnie Smith, with whom he had played a couple of gigs, urged Elvis to see Eddie Bond, leader of a band Smith belonged to; there was an opening for a vocalist. After the tryout, Bond advised Elvis to stick with truck driving.

"You're never going to make it as a singer," Bond said.

Elvis Presley could have been driving a truck his

whole life. Think about it: The King of Rock 'n' Roll could have been a truck driver, singing to himself instead of to his millions of fans. He marched to the beat of a different drum – and not to the chorus of negative voices that tried to tell him he didn't have the talent to be a professional singer.

*   *   *

Albert Einstein:
A slow learner?

Considered by many to be one of the most brilliant minds in the world of science, Albert Einstein didn't get off to a very promising start in life.

Observing that he seemed to have a lot of difficulty speaking before the age of two, the family maid referred to him as "the dopey one." Some in his immediate family labeled him as "almost backwards." His sister wondered if he would ever learn to speak properly, given the trouble he had talking fluently as a youngster. His parents took him to the doctor to see what was wrong with him.

Einstein biographer Walter Isaacson tells us that very early in life Einstein exhibited a "rebelliousness toward authority" which, combined with his slow development, "led one schoolmaster to send him packing and another to amuse history by declaring that he would never amount to much."

Despite widely held myths to the contrary, Einstein's grades in school were outstanding, even in subjects for which he had little liking.

"He disliked the mechanical learning of languages such as Latin and Greek, a problem exacerbated by what he later said was his 'bad memory for words and texts,'" according to Isaacson. "(When he was 15) his general outlook toward received wisdom... inculcated an allergic reaction against all forms of dogma and authority."

At 15, Einstein dropped out of school and returned to his parents' home, promising to study on his own. His rebelliousness effectively blocked the efforts of the system, or of any individual representing it, to define him or his destiny. He remained a rebellious outsider all his life, and as a result endured much rejection.

Einstein searched for employment as a professor after graduation from Zurich Polytechnic, sending out numerous letters and résumés to various European universities, all to no avail.

Failing to secure an academic position, he took a job in the local patent office. When he wasn't on duty in his day job, he ambitiously pursued his scientific studies.

In May 1905, Einstein wrote to a friend about his scientific research plans. He promised four papers, including one about the electrodynamics of moving bodies. This study gave birth to his Special Theory of Relativity, $E=mc^2$ – "the best-known equation in all of physics," according to Isaacson.

By early 1908, Einstein was still employed at the patent office, without success in his quest for an academic position. Having given up on becoming a university professor, he resigned himself to working as a high school teacher. So, he applied for a job to teach math and geometry at a high school in Zurich and even enclosed his papers on his Special Theory of Relativity. But he was not hired.

At long last, in 1909, at the age of 30, he was offered a position as a junior professor at the University of Zurich, a job which he began in October of that year.

In conclusion, had Albert Einstein's ambitions sunk under the weight of repeated rejection and discouragement – had he succumbed to the will and definitions of others – we may never have heard of the Theory of Relativity, and our perception of the world in which we live would be significantly different.

To be sure, Einstein was blessed with a uniquely huge intellectual capacity. He also possessed an extraordinary will to succeed – without which his intellect would never have found its full expression.

The story of Einstein's life teaches tenacity in the face of rejection. The overriding message of his story, as it relates to our first hurdle of life, is this: Don't let any group or anyone control your destiny.

Had Albert Einstein allowed the experts in charge to control his destiny, the destiny of our world would be very different, and the worse for it.

* * *

Walt Disney: The very bumpy road to success

It's hard not to admire Walt Disney.

The man built an entertainment empire. Long after his passing, his name and signature still stand today as one of the most recognizable brands and logos in the world.

His characters – once figments of his remark-able, imaginative mind – have stood the test of time. Mickey Mouse has entertained generations of children – and more than just a few grown-ups, for that matter.

Disneyland in California and Disney World in Florida are monuments to this man's accomplish-ments.

And he achieved it all while overcoming one of the most common hurdles of life: "I can't" and "You can't." He seems to have had an ironclad faith that he'd get over all the obstacles life put in his path.

One of the most fascinating things I discovered while learning about the life of Disney is how often he was told, in so many words, "You can't." Luckily for the rest of us who admire his creations, he never listened to the naysayers, the voices of discouragement.

In fact, Walt Disney's success story is packed with disappointment, defeat, rejection, bankruptcy, betrayal and loss. But Disney – driven by a powerful urge to keep exploring, to keep trying – overcame all these hurdles.

His initial aspirations in the art world were modest.

At the age of 18, after a tour of duty in World War I as a driver for the Red Cross, he wanted to be an editorial cartoonist for *The Kansas City Star*. To do so, he knew he needed to land a job with *The Star*, to get a toe in the door – even if it meant starting as a janitor. When an opening for office boy arose, Disney applied, but his application was rejected.

So, he accepted an apprenticeship producing ads at a downtown Kansas City print shop. He worked through the Christmas advertising rush before being laid off. Next, he landed a job at the post office, delivering mail for a short period of time.

Disney then got a job at the Kansas City Slide Company, the biggest mail order slide company in the nation. The owner was also in the business of making filmed ads – animated ads – an art form that fascinated Disney. Here was a chance to get in on the ground floor of something exciting. So, Disney's place of employment became his art school. He spent countless hours learning the techniques of animation.

Then he set up his own studio, behind the house where he lived, to experiment and practice making animated cartoons. He made several and called them "Laugh-O-Grams" and sold them to local theaters.

The Laugh-O-Grams were a hit, so Disney started his own company, Laugh-O-Gram Films, Inc. However, the enterprise proved to be unprofitable as he searched in vain for a distributor. The company sank into debt and ended in bankruptcy.

Though his company failed, Disney did produce a notable work called *Alice's Wonderland*. He left Kansas City on a train bound for Hollywood with his only copy of the film in his suitcase. He hoped to find a film distributor in Hollywood, but that didn't pan out.

He then submitted the reel to a New York animation distribution company, which contracted with him to make more films. So, he and his brother, Roy, got a rich uncle to loan them money to set up a studio in Hollywood. There they made several more episodes in the *Alice* series.

Next, Disney created a new character, Oswald, the Lucky Rabbit, which received favorable reviews. But he neglected to secure the rights to the character and ended up having a falling out with the owners of the distribution company.

After meeting with them in New York, and realizing he had lost control of his own creation, Disney was quite upset. He felt he had gotten a raw deal.

But before he boarded the train to return to Hollywood, he began to draw a character to replace Oswald the Lucky Rabbit. His new creation: a mouse.

The story goes that "somewhere between Chicago and Los Angeles...Disney wrote a scenario for a cartoon he called *Plane Crazy*, about a mouse who – inspired by Charles Lindbergh's 1927 solo flight over the Atlantic Ocean – builds himself a plane to impress a lady mouse."

The mouse Walt drew was long and skinny. But in Hollywood one of his associates redesigned the mouse, making him short and round, and called him Mickey – Mickey Mouse.

Disney, of course, hung on to the rights to this fresh new character, thinking that perhaps Mickey would be his ticket to a bright future.

Thus, another hurdle was cleared – a life-altering hurdle – and Walt Disney was now on his way to a level of success as a cartoon animator that would prove to be beyond his wildest imagination.

*   *   *

Rudy Ruettiger:
The Heart of the Fighting Irish

The University of Notre Dame football program has produced some well-known athletes, but none more famous than a guy named Rudy.

Though he wasn't seen on the field very much, Rudy Ruettiger was looked upon with great admiration by many of his teammates and the fans who came to regard him as the Heart of the Fighting Irish.

Rudy's dream of playing for Notre Dame started when he was a kid and turned into a passion in his teenage years. He thought about it all the time. He would imagine himself dressed out in the handsome blue and gold uniform, the crowd cheering as he caught the game-winning pass and scurried into the end zone.

But the problem was, he was just a little guy, short, light weight and not particularly gifted as an athlete. Another problem was that hardly anyone else believed he would be a college football player.

He was the third of 14 children in a blue collar family growing up in Joliet, Illinois. So money would be an issue for gaining admission to Notre Dame. His parents would say on more than one occasion, "You can't go because we can't afford it." Then there was the question of his academic qualifications. He wasn't a great student and he struggled to earn even mid-range grades. He would find out later in life that what made school so difficult was that he had a learning disability called dyslexia.

But, regardless, Rudy wanted to go to Notre Dame and play football.

His motivation was simple: He wanted to be somebody, to do something worthwhile with his life.

"In the culture I grew up in – in a blue collar family, with 14 children, in the Midwest – if you went to Notre Dame you were somebody," he explained.

After high school, rather than apply for entry to Notre Dame right away, Rudy joined the Navy and served for two years.

"When I joined the Navy I was surrounded by people who built me up," Rudy explains. "They identified my strengths – character, commitment and loyalty – and built on that. They saw me as someone they could count on, and they treated me as such.

"As a result, the low sense of self-esteem I had as a teenager took on a whole new life; it got healthier because it was clear to see that someone believed in me besides just me."

Because of his military service, Rudy was eligible for the G.I. Bill, which provides financial aid for college. But he wasn't quite ready to apply for entry into college, so he worked for a year or so at the power plant where his father, brother and best friend worked, saving some of his earnings to help with college expenses.

While on the job, something terrible happened: His best friend – the one guy who supported him in his hope of playing football for Notre Dame – was killed in an explosion at the plant.

"That was the turning point for me – the catalyst that got me going. I decided to take concrete steps right away to pursue my dreams," Rudy says.

"The sudden death of my friend showed me that life is too short. I didn't want to live in regret for the rest of my life, wishing I had played for Notre Dame. So, I decided to go for it! I realized that if I tried and failed, at least I would know I tried my best and would never have to look back on my life thinking I never went for it while I had the chance."

In 1972, he applied for admission to Notre Dame but was turned down. One of the administrators at Notre Dame, a Holy Cross brother, saw how earnestly Rudy wanted to attend, so he suggested an alternative plan: Enroll at nearby Holy Cross College – a small school just across the street from Notre Dame – then re-apply after a year or two.

Rudy took the brother's advice and completed two years at Holy Cross. While there, he applied three more times for admission to Notre Dame and was finally accepted in the fall of 1974.

It was now time to try out for the football team. Luckily for Rudy, the head coach at the time, Ara

Parseghian, welcomed walk-ons.

So, Rudy walked on, tried out, and made the team!

At least, he made the practice squad, which meant that, barring some extraordinary circumstances, he would never dress out for the games.

But that was okay with him, because he could now say he was one of the Fighting Irish of Notre Dame. His dream had become his reality.

"I was fine with being on the practice squad," he would say later. "It's the way that I was able to be on the team and contribute to its success. I felt I could help make the team better in this way."

Rudy was, indeed, in the thick of things as a Notre Dame football player. He suited up every day, never missing a practice. He played as a defensive lineman, taking on men who outweighed him by 100 pounds and who towered over him by 12 inches. He weighed 190 and stood 5-foot-6. It was like David versus Goliath. He did get banged up – bloody nose, cut lip, bruised elbows, sprained ankle – but was never seriously injured.

Rudy hung in there and played with a lot of heart. Dan Devine – the coach who replaced Ara Parseghian the season after Rudy joined the team – said to his team that they'd have a better record if everyone played with the heart and hustle that Rudy displayed every day. So, Rudy did contribute to the betterment of the team, and his teammates respected him for it.

If Rudy hustled during practice, he worked just as hard off the field – at his studies and at his various income-producing jobs. He helped to clean up the football stadium after games and the basketball arena after various events; he also worked as a night-time security guard. He managed to get free room and board, living in the athletic center and eating with the other players.

For the last game of his college career, Rudy was allowed to dress out and to play a couple of plays in the fourth quarter. To the chants of the crowd – "Ru-dy, Ru-dy, Ru-dy" – he ran onto the field and lined up at left defensive end. On the final play of the game, Rudy got through the line, sprinted to the Georgia Tech quarterback, and sacked him.

The crowd erupted in wild applause and cheering, and Rudy's teammates picked him up, put him on their shoulders, and carried him off the field. What a glorious moment that must have been for Rudy Ruettiger – the Heart of the Fighting Irish.

Some years later, Rudy was asked how he managed to hang on to his dream in spite of all the discouraging messages from those around him.

"I didn't get mad at the naysayers. I just withdrew from them. And when I did hear the doubting words, I didn't take them to heart. I had an energy around me that their words could not penetrate," he explained. "I turned a deaf ear to what they were saying."

*   *   *

After graduation from Notre Dame, with a degree in sociology, Rudy worked as a graduate assistant while pursuing a second degree. He didn't get that second degree, but instead headed out into the world to make a living. He sold insurance and worked for auto dealerships in South Bend, Indiana. He also started a cleaning company, built it up, and sold it before returning to insurance sales.

All the while, Rudy was harboring a dream about a project that could prove to be almost as exciting as playing football for the Irish: a movie based on his experiences at Notre Dame. He felt his story was interesting enough and that it taught valuable lessons about perseverance, positive thinking and following one's dream.

So, in 1982 he began a quest to have a big screen movie made based on his life story. Naturally, along the way he bumped into numerous Hollywood naysayers who used language similar to what he had heard in his youth: "You can't. It won't work. We already have enough football stories. It wouldn't draw enough of an audience to make it commercially viable."

Turns out, the experts were mistaken. The movie was made and released in 1993.

It's called *Rudy*.

It was a box office sensation and is now considered one of the 50 most popular movies of all time. It has sold literally millions of copies in DVD format. Adults all over the U.S. play it for their children, and adults play it for themselves when they want to lift their spirits.

Today, Rudy is a motivational speaker who addresses audiences young and old, students, athletes and businesspeople. He talks to them about doing their best, overcoming obstacles, not being afraid to fail, and getting up after getting knocked down.

He never tells an audience, "You can't," as he heard so many times as a young man.

Instead, the theme of many of his talks is, "Yes, I can."

Chapter 6

The Second Hurdle:
Past failures / Fear of failure

ear of failure blocks success in a world that is abundant with opportunity. But successful people know that success is often built on failure.

Take former UCLA Coach John Wooden, for example. He coached his basketball teams to ten NCAA Championships – far more than any other coach. But his teams did not even make it into the Final Four until he was midway through his 27-year tenure at UCLA. Nowadays, at a school like UCLA, he might have been fired for that level of failure.

Five times John Wooden's teams lost in the NCAA tournament's first round. Undeterred, he recognized that success often follows failure and that failure can drive success.

Coach Wooden and his teams continued to work hard. Finally, in his sixteenth year as head coach they won the National Championship. And they continued to win it. In all, they won the championship in 10 of Coach Wooden's last 12 years at UCLA.

The first lesson here is that you can't let your past failures define you. When I was growing up, the people I learned the most from were people who refused to be unduly affected by their mistakes. They didn't crumble when they failed; they learned and grew stronger as a result.

The successes of many well-known and influential people were built on failures. For instance, President Abraham Lincoln failed in business and was defeated in his bids to become a legislator and later to become a U.S. Senator for the State of Illinois. His successes were grounded in the wisdom he acquired from his failures.

Gen. Douglas MacArthur applied for admission to West Point and was denied more than once. Each denial strengthened his resolve to succeed.

J.K. Rowling's manuscript for the first of her *Harry Potter* books was rejected by several publishers. She too gathered strength from past failures.

Steven Spielberg, one of the most talented and successful American movie directors ever, was turned down for admission to the University of Southern California School of Theater, Film and Television. Nor was he accepted into the UCLA film school.

The very different stories of Lincoln, MacArthur, Rowling and Spielberg have in common their demonstration that past failures can generate persistence and an extraordinary will to succeed. Moreover, their refusal to be defeated in their endeavors made a significant and enduring difference for the better in their own lives and in the lives of millions of others.

* * *

Just as failure can strengthen the will to succeed, it can also sometimes bring about a crippling level of guilt. Now, guilt comes easier to some than to others; it tends to remain longer with some than with others.

And here we need to be careful not to shackle ourselves with feelings of guilt for long periods of time, for guilt can lead to the suffocation of one's spirit. It can fester like a wound that won't heal and can cause aggression, depression, self-doubt, and a litany of other negative consequences.

We've got to learn to forgive ourselves. If we're going to live truly productive lives, we must quit beating ourselves up with thoughts of "I should have done this, I could have done that, I really dropped the ball...."

None of us will ever see the day when we can plan our performance and manage our behavior to perfection. It's not going to happen. We're all going to fall short from time to time.

One effective approach to dealing with guilt – and

putting it behind us – is this: Acknowledge our failure or shortcoming, resolve to do better next time, forgive ourselves, seek forgiveness of others if the situation warrants it, then just move on.

It helps, too, to recall the wise and reassuring words of two well-known authors.

Oliver Wendell Holmes wrote, "What lies behind you and what lies ahead of you are of little importance when compared to what lies within you."

Oscar Wilde wrote, "Every saint has a past and every sinner has a future."

Most of us fall in the latter category, so take heart!

*   *   *

J.K. Rowling:
On the benefits of failure

In early summer of 2008, renowned author J.K. Rowling delivered the commencement address at Harvard University. She was 42 at the time and at the peak of her success as the writer of the wildly popular *Harry Potter* book series. Ironically, her talk was on the benefits of failure.

She said to her audience that as a child she told stories to her younger sister, Di, and even then had set her sights on being a writer. As a teenager in the mid-1980s, she had a "serious ambition to be a writer."

By October 2000, her success warranted an appearance on *Larry King Live*. That year, *The Goblet of Fire*, the fourth Potter book, had sold nearly 400,000 copies the first day in the U.K., nearly equal to the number her third book sold in an entire year.

"I've been writing since I was six years old.... I'll be writing until I can't write anymore. It's a compulsion with me. I love writing," she told Larry King.

Harry Potter and the Deathly Hallows, the seventh and last of the series, was released in July of 2007 and sold eleven million copies the first day in the United Kingdom and the United States. All told, by the end of 2007 her books had sold some 400 million copies and had been translated into more than 60 languages. She was a billionaire.

As she stood before her audience to deliver the Harvard commencement address, she was arguably the planet's most successful and widely read living author.

"A mere seven years after my graduation day, I had failed on an epic scale. An exceptionally short-lived marriage had imploded, and I was jobless, a lone parent, and as poor as it is possible to be in modern Britain without being homeless.... I was the biggest failure I knew," she confessed.

The idea for Harry Potter came to Jo in 1990.

"It simply fell into my head," she recalled.

She was on the train returning to London from

Manchester. Traveling alone, she did not have a pen and "was too shy to ask anybody if I could borrow one."

"This was probably a good thing, because I simply sat and thought, for four (delayed train) hours, and all the details bubbled up in my brain, and this scrawny, black-haired, bespectacled boy who didn't know he was a wizard became more and more real to me. I think that if I had had to slow down the ideas so that I could capture them on paper I might have stifled some of them," she said.

Now back in London, she began writing *The Philosopher's Stone* "that very evening."

Later that same year, after a ten-year illness her mother died of multiple sclerosis at the age of 45. Jo was devastated.

Nine months later, to get away, she moved to Portugal, where she taught English in a language institute and pressed on with her novel. While there, she married a Portuguese man and had a daughter. But the marriage wasn't working so well, so she divorced her husband and went to stay with her sister, Di, in Edinburgh.

She planned to begin teaching again, but she knew that unless she finished the book very soon, she might never finish it.

"Full-time teaching, with all the marking and lesson planning, let alone with a small daughter to care for single-handedly, would leave me with absolutely no spare time at all…. And so I set to work in a kind of frenzy, determined to finish the book and at least try and get it published," she related.

Altogether the manuscript was five years in the making. When it was finally done, she sent the first three chapters off to an agent, who promptly returned her package. The second agent she tried wrote back asking to see the rest of the manuscript. Jo was ecstatic.

It took her new agent a year to find a publisher; several publishers rejected the manuscript, but in August 1996 Bloomsbury made an offer.

"So why do I talk about the benefits of failure?"

The question must have seemed ironic to her audience since, for most of them, no doubt, J.K. Rowling personified the hope for success and fulfillment harbored by the new graduates and their parents. She answered her own question:

"Simply because failure meant a stripping away of the inessential. I stopped pretending to myself that I was anything other than what I was, and I began to direct all my energy into finishing the only work that mattered to me. Had I really succeeded at anything else, I might never have found the determination to succeed in the one arena I believed I truly belonged. I was set free because my greatest fear had been realized, and I was still alive, and I still had a daughter whom I adored, and I had an old typewriter and a big idea. And so rock bottom became the solid foundation on which I built my life."

At that rock bottom, there had been nothing for Jo to do but write.

"Failure taught me things about myself that I could have learned no other way. I discovered that I had a strong will, and more discipline than I had suspected; I also found out that I had friends whose value was truly above the price of rubies....

"The knowledge that you have emerged wiser and stronger from setbacks means that you are, ever after, secure in your ability to survive. You will never truly know yourself, or the strength of your relationships, until both have been tested by adversity."

She made it clear that she believed – based on her own experience – that success and happiness can be built on failure.

"It's impossible to live without failing at something, unless you live so cautiously that you might as well not have lived at all – in which case, you fail by default," she said.

For Jo Rowling, the happiness that flowed from success ultimately came from knowing she could survive adversity and failure. She doubted she could have reached the success and happiness she now enjoys had she not experienced failure.

*   *   *

Steven Spielberg:
He kept failing to get into film school

He may go down in history as the most talented American movie director of all time, but Steven Spielberg failed to gain admission to California film schools on several occasions in his younger days.

Spielberg directed several of the most commercially successful films of our time: *Jaws*, *E.T.*, *Jurassic Park* and *Indiana Jones*. But he was unsuccessful in his quest for admission to the UCLA film school. He was also turned down by the University of Southern California School of Theater, Film, and Television.

Spielberg was an indifferent student in high school, absorbed as he was in his passion for films. As a teenager he made 8 mm adventure films, including staged wrecks with his electric train. He charged 25 cents to see the show, while his sister sold popcorn. In 1958, he fulfilled the requirements for the photography merit badge in the Boy Scouts by making *The Last Gunfight*, a nine-minute 8 mm film.

In 1965, having failed in repeated attempts to gain admission to the top film schools of UCLA and USC, he enrolled at California State University at Long Beach. He attended for three years before leaving to pursue his filmmaking career. Long after he had achieved success as a maker of films, he returned to complete his degree.

In May 2002, he received his Bachelor's degree from California State University at Long Beach. He used the occasion to thank his parents for their support and to joke about the amount of time it took to get his degree.

"I wanted to accomplish this for many years as a 'thank you' to my parents for giving me the opportunity for an education and a career, and as a personal note for my own family – and young people everywhere – about the importance of achieving their college education goals.

"But I hope they get there quicker than I did. Completing the requirements for my degree 33 years after finishing my principal education marks my longest 'post-production' schedule," he said.

By then Spielberg had received three Academy Awards, two for producing and directing *Schindler's List* and one for directing *The Color Purple*. He had also received the Lifetime Achievement Award from the Directors Guild.

Spielberg's repeated failures to get into film schools more than three decades earlier were certainly frustrating, but, as it turned out, he did okay for himself!

And he never let his failures define him.

Chapter 7

The Third Hurdle: Handicaps

For many of us, when we hear the word "handicapped" we automatically think of people whose handicaps are obvious and clear-cut. We may think of the soldier in a wheelchair who lost his legs on the battlefield; or the woman who drives into the handicapped parking space and struggles noticeably to walk a short distance; or perhaps a child who was born with Down syndrome.

However, the truth is that there are handicapped people all around us, all the time, whose handicaps are not so easily detectable. In our everyday lives, we see people who are handicapped psychologically, emotionally, financially and in terms of their jobs and careers. They may be lonely, under severe financial stress, trapped by various circumstances, possibly without friends or family who can help them, and seemingly without hope for a better life.

Most of us have handicaps of one kind or another. We are encumbered by disadvantages that seem to block our way to a happy and fulfilling life. Now, these handicaps can become crutches that we lean on to excuse our lack of success and happiness.

We tell ourselves and others, "I'm an immigrant, I'm uneducated, I'm shy, I'm sick, I'm poor, I was abused, I'm not smart enough, I never knew my father, I was an orphan, I have no connections." The list is long; it may take in all of life's circumstances in one way or another.

These disadvantages are real, not merely imagined or concocted to get us off the hook for our failed efforts – or, what is worse, for our failure to put forth the necessary effort. But if we are going to improve our lot in life, what counts most is not our background or our circumstances – both of which may be beyond our control – but our "backbone": grit, determination, strength of will, belief in ourselves.

Sometimes handicaps, or disadvantages, result from injury or disease that can deprive us of control over our life's outcomes. Something happens that brings us up short of our expectations and dreams; something happens that darkens our future. So, we despair. *How can I win against such odds? Why even try?* We withdraw from the field of battle and concede the victory to the forces, outer and inner, stacked up against us.

Overcoming a disadvantage means turning it into an advantage and regaining control in some way that counts, in spite of our reduced range of abilities. Of course, there are things we cannot control, such as accidental injury, illness, or the absence of a parent. The odds against us may seem insurmountable. But even in the worst of circumstances, there are some things we can control, and these are what we need to discover and turn to our advantage. Indeed, in our confrontation with such obstacles, we discover abilities within us that we may not have known we had.

I have a mental list of famous and not-so-famous people who did just that, who by turning a negative into a positive overcame great handicaps, seemingly impassable obstacles, on the way to remarkable and valuable achievements. For example:

• Paul Anderson, who as a child was diagnosed with terminal kidney disease and who was not expected to live past age 12, built himself up to be an Olympic Gold Medal weightlifter and became literally "the strongest man in the world."

• Kay Vandiver, a right-handed bowler who lost her right arm in an auto accident, discovered within herself the will and fortitude to return to bowling, and not only to return but to win.

• Bill W., who was handicapped by chronic drunkenness and turmoil in his personal affairs, finally achieved sobriety and serenity. After years of depression, frustration, and near-despair, he became the co-founder of Alcoholics Anonymous, an organization that has helped millions of men and women all over the world to stop drinking.

• Oprah Winfrey was born into poverty in rural Mississippi, sexually abused as a child, and pregnant at age 14. But she worked her way into a new life in the broadcast media, later hosting her own TV show and becoming a movie actor, magazine publisher and billionaire philanthropist. She was described by *Forbes* Magazine as "the richest self-made woman in America" and was named several times by *TIME* Magazine as "one of America's most influential people."

In the face of a handicap of any kind – if we have cultivated and maintained a positive vision of life – we can uncover capacities within us that otherwise would have remained dormant. These capacities can empower us to succeed in our pursuit of a life that is both fulfilling and joyful.

*   *   *

Paul Anderson: 'The strongest man in the world'

Paul Anderson was the strongest man in the world.

What a man! They called him the "Dixie Derrick,"

perhaps in part because he could lift two 55-gallon drums filled with water and suspended by ropes from a bar across his shoulders.

He was born in Toccoa, Georgia, in 1932. When he was five years old he was diagnosed with Bright's disease, named for the British physician who, in 1827, was the first to identify the disease's primary symptoms. The term "Bright's disease" is now obsolete, but it was used then to identify a variety of kidney diseases, which today would be called nephritis. Among the symptoms are the presence of albumin in the urine, severe back pain, abdominal pain, fatigue, and hypertension.

Paul's parents were called to the hospital, where the doctor gave them the bad news. He said Paul would be seriously handicapped by this dreaded disease, unable to handle most of the everyday physical activities enjoyed by his healthier classmates. He predicted that by age 12 Paul would die from kidney failure.

Paul was there and heard what the doctor told his parents. Though he was only a child at the time, he refused to believe what the doctor said.

Bright's disease is a serious condition that is progressive and eventually results in renal failure. However, there is a long list of people who were afflicted with this disease who nevertheless achieved notable success. These include Chester Arthur, the twenty-first President of the United States; Emily Dickinson, the nineteenth century American poet, whose poems are still read in American literature classes by high school and college students; and – perhaps the most important to Paul Anderson – Canadian strongman Louis Cyr, who in 1895 lifted on his back 18 men on a platform, a lift of 4,337 pounds.

Disregarding the doctor's doomsday prediction, or perhaps in defiance of it, young Paul Anderson decided he was going to build himself up. Growing up in the Georgia hills in a poor family, Paul started lifting weights.

Now, these were not the standard barbells and dumbbells you'd expect to find in a high school gym. These were of the homemade variety. He made cylindrical chunks of concrete in buckets and car tires and attached them to the ends of discarded car axles. This is what he lifted at first; though they weren't stylish, they apparently worked pretty well. As we see, where there's a will, there's a way!

As a teenager, he aspired to be the fullback on his high school football team. He not only got to be his high school's starting fullback but also won a football scholarship to Furman University in Greenville, South Carolina, where he got into serious weightlifting.

Although he stood only 5-foot-9, he eventually built up to 375 pounds – with a 62-inch chest and 36-inch thighs. He found he had extraordinary strength in his legs. While still a freshman at Furman he squatted more than 400 pounds – at the time considered fantastic for so young an athlete.

He left Furman during his freshman year and went to his parents' home – now in Elizabethton, Tennessee – where the legendary weightlifter Bob Peoples discovered Paul and encouraged him to enter the world of competitive weightlifting.

In 1952 – now eight years beyond the doctor's prognosis of his death – he competed in the Tennessee state weightlifting championships and established heavyweight records in the overhead press, snatch, and clean-and-jerk. He also did a 660-pound squat. At the 1955 national championships in Cleveland, Ohio, Anderson lifted 436 pounds in the clean-and-jerk for a world record. Later that year he competed in an international event in Moscow, as the USA National Amateur Union Weightlifting Champion. Newsreel narrator Bud Palmer described the scene:

"Then up to the bar stepped a great ball of a man, Paul Anderson."

The bar was set at 402.5 pounds. The Russian champion had just matched the world record press of 330.5 pounds. The narrator observed that the Russians snickered as Anderson gripped the bar – but they cheered when he pressed it over his head, pressing more weight than anyone in history. *Chudo piryody* ("a wonder of nature!"), the awestruck Russians shouted.

In Munich, Germany, Anderson pressed 407.7

pounds on the way to breaking two world records. He won a gold medal in the super-heavyweight class in the 1956 Olympics in Melbourne, Australia.

After the 1956 Olympic Games, Anderson turned professional and started accepting payment for weightlifting exhibitions.

His most incredible feat was the back-lift. The back-lift is an event you don't see much in the United States. The weight is placed on a table or flat surface of some sort; in many cases the weight is that of people sitting or standing on a wooden platform. The weightlifter hunches under the platform and straightens up, using mainly the strength of his thighs to lift the weight. (Louis Cyr had set the world record of 4,337 pounds in 1895.) Anderson's unbelievable back-lift of 6,270 pounds – the weight of a small bull elephant – earned him a spot in the *Guinness Book of World Records*.

Imagine, the boy who was not supposed to live past the age of 12 – handicapped by a painful and debilitating disease of the kidneys – breaking a world record in weightlifting that had stood for more than half a century. And he broke the record by nearly 2,000 pounds!

*　　*　　*

I was a high school coach in Minot, North Dakota, in 1960 when I heard that Paul Anderson would be in Estes Park, Colorado, to speak. I saved up as much money as I could to make the trip, two states away from where I was. As a coach, I wanted to know what made this man so strong. How did he do it?

I arrived early at the place where he was to speak. I was on the front row, right in the middle. The auditorium filled up fast. The announcer came out and stood behind the podium. On stage beside the podium, the hosts had set up two sawhorses, with a two-by-four laid across them.

"Ladies and gentlemen," the announcer said, "Paul Anderson, the strongest man in the world."

A great ball of a man – exactly as Bud Palmer had described him when he was competing in the weight-lifting event in Moscow in the mid-1950s – waddled out onto the stage. When you saw him, you could believe he was capable of lifting a bull elephant on his back.

But what he did then was just as unbelievable. Without saying a word, he took a white, neatly folded handkerchief and a ten-penny nail from the podium and went over to the sawhorses with the two-by-four laid across them. He shook out the handkerchief so everybody could see it was just a handkerchief and placed it in the palm of his right hand. He took the nail in that hand, point outward between the fingers of his clenched fist. He raised his hand arm's-length high and then – *bam!* – slammed his fist down on the board, driving the nail through the two-by-four so that about an inch of it protruded from the bottom side.

What we saw was what we saw – no tricks, no sleight of hand, no optical illusion. He slowly came around to the microphone, where he leaned forward a little toward the audience. In his gravel voice – exactly the voice you'd expect from a man who looked like Paul Anderson and who had done what he had done – he said:

"Good morning. My name is Paul Anderson. I am, I am the strongest man in the history of the world. There's no one stronger than me."

Then he lowered his voice to just above a whisper, barely audible through the mic, and added:

"And I cannot live one day without God."

Displays of physical strength, however awesome, do not tell the whole story of Paul Anderson. His display of physical power that day in Estes Park was incredible, but it served at the same time as a testament to his ironclad faith in God. Strong as he was – his "lifelong tug-of-war with kidneys" severely damaged by Bright's disease notwithstanding – he claimed no personal credit. Instead, he attributed his many successes and indeed his sheer survival to "the Lord." With nine world records and an Olympic gold medal, his source of strength was not his training methods but his faith, and his commitment to be a servant of God. That was his message.

In 1961 he and his wife Glenda founded the

— White House photo

Oprah Winfrey, handicapped by an awful childhood that included sexual abuse by relatives, got into broadcasting at a young age and rose to become one of the most powerful women in the U.S.

Bill W., handicapped by chronic drunkenness, was the co-founder of Alcoholics Anonymous, helping millions of men and women all over the world to stop drinking.

— Photo courtesy of the Paul Anderson Youth Home

Paul Anderson, "the strongest man in the world," works out with homemade weights built with a car axle and cement set in tires. He was handicapped by a terminal kidney disease, which he refused to allow to rule his life. Doctors said he would die by age 12; he lived to be 61.

Walt Disney, creator of Mickey Mouse and Disneyland, got off to a shaky start as a cartoon animator, going broke at age 21.

Albert Einstein, referred to early in life as "the dopey one," wrote the best-known equation in all of physics, $E=mc^2$.

Elvis Presley, "King of Rock 'n' Roll," was told he didn't have the voice to be a singer, and that he'd better stick to truck driving.

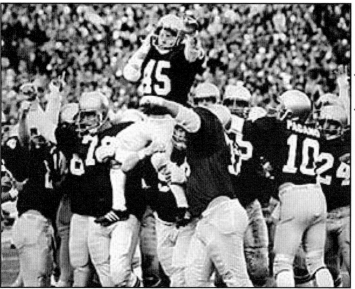

– Photos courtesy of Rudy International

Rudy Ruettiger refused to listen to the voices of his detractors who said he'd never make the Notre Dame football team. **Above:** *Rudy is carried off the field after playing in the first and only game of his college career, in the fall of 1976.* **Left:** *Today, Rudy is a much-sought-after motivational speaker who tells his audiences that the obstacles to success can be overcome in part by maintaining a positive mental attitude, by working hard, and by staying away from those who would discourage you rather than encourage you toward your goals.*

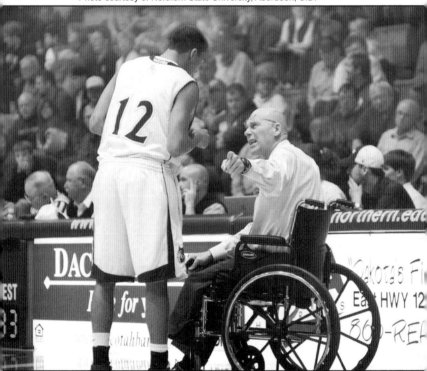

Don Meyer, head coach of the Northern State University basketball team in Aberdeen, S.D., coaches from his wheelchair after losing a leg in a near-fatal car crash. Doctors doubted he'd ever walk or coach again. After 55 days in the hospital, he was back at work at 4:45 the next morning. He went on to become the winningest coach in U.S. college basketball history, with 923 victories.

– Photo courtesy of LSU Sports Information

Shaquille O'Neal was cut from his high school basketball team in 1985, supposedly for a lack of talent and stamina. Later, he blossomed as an athlete while playing for LSU. He was the No. 1 pick in the NBA draft following his junior year and was voted NBA Rookie of the Year in 1993. He played for five teams in his 19-year pro career, retiring in 2011 as one of the top 50 NBA players of all time.

– Photo courtesy of the Boston Celtics

Steven Spielberg, one of the most accomplished movie directors in the history of American cinema, was turned down repeatedly in his effort to gain admission to the top film schools in California.

J.K. Rowling, who once referred to herself as "the biggest failure I knew," succeeded to a phenomenal degree when she wrote the Harry Potter series of books. Though her first manuscript was rejected by several publishers, her 7-book series went on to sell some 400 million copies and turned her into a billionaire.

▲ John Wooden, former head basketball coach of the UCLA Bruins and winner of 10 NCAA Championships, got off to a less-than-stellar start in his 27-year tenure at UCLA. That's me on the right, expressing my love and respect for the man who was my mentor for the better part of 40 years.

◀ My mom, Agnes Brown, and me at home in Minot, N.D., circa 1939. I grew up in poverty in a 1-room apartment and was well-prepared to take on life's adversities and challenges, thanks in large part to my mom's wisdom and counsel.

"Pistol Pete" Maravich, who may have been the greatest basketball player who ever lived, played for LSU from 1966 to 1970, then went on to a successful and lucrative NBA career. Despite the adulation heaped upon him, deep down he was "a miserable human being," as he said publicly on several occasions. He even considered suicide once but was reprieved by a spiritual awakening. In time, he came to know his true self – including who he was in relationship to God. He went on to be something of an evangelist, urging his audiences to turn to God and away from the kind of materialism and narcissism that nearly did him in.

Paul Anderson Youth Home, a "Christian home for troubled and homeless young men between the ages of 16 and 21, the majority of whom may otherwise be sentenced to penal institutions." Relinquishing his amateur status to become a professional athlete allowed Anderson to support the home with funds from his lifting exhibitions and speaking engagements. These numbered in the hundreds annually and occurred at churches, civic clubs, high schools, colleges, businesses, industries, and military bases. A lifter of spirits, he spoke about his belief in Jesus Christ, family values, patriotism, and the American free enterprise system.

He was very active as a public speaker for quite a number of years – until he suffered renal failure in 1983. His sister Dorothy gave him one of her kidneys, which prolonged his life for eleven years. He died in 1994 at the age of 61.

A news reporter who spent some time with the Andersons, especially observing their work with the Youth Home, said of Paul:

"He is the world's strongest man, and he also lifts weights."

I think often of the day I saw Paul Anderson in Estes Park, Colorado. I will never forget him and the way he overcame his physical "handicap," getting over this seemingly insurmountable hurdle to become the strongest man in the world.

His amazing display of strength and his simple

message about the power of faith affected me profoundly. The Paul Anderson story – what he stood for, what he had to teach us all about faith, courage and tenacity – has driven me my entire adult life.

*   *   *

Kay Vandiver:
The gal just wanted to bowl!

Kay Vandiver was an outstanding young bowler who lived in Devil's Lake, North Dakota, not far from where I grew up.

In 1961, she traveled to Minneapolis, Minnesota, to compete in one of the world's largest women's bowling tournaments. In the final game of the tournament she bowled a perfect 300 and won the championship.

To say only that she was excited would be an understatement. She was ecstatic. Here she was, an amateur, from a small town, competing against not only amateurs but also world-ranked professionals. And she won. Now she could quit her ordinary little job in Devil's Lake and become a professional bowler.

But then, suddenly, disaster.

After receiving her trophy, she was driving home at night and she ran into a train.

It was a terrible accident. Severely injured, Kay was pinned in the wreckage for four and a half hours before rescuers could get her out. The ambulance rushed her to the hospital. Her parents were called and told to come to the hospital immediately. They were told the doctors did not expect Kay to live through the night. Her right arm was badly crushed. The surgeon had to amputate it – the arm with which she had just bowled the perfect 300 game.

Kay was in a coma for three months and would remain in the hospital for two years. Four times her parents were called to hurry back to her hospital bedside because her death seemed imminent. But through each crisis she somehow managed to hang on to life.

Her recovery was painfully slow. With assistance and with tremendous effort, one day she sat up. As the days went by she was able to sit up for longer periods of time. One day she managed to put her foot on the floor. Later, she got her other foot on the floor. Then she got up out of bed. After a while, she was able to sit in the chair beside her bed. Next, she took a step or two, then several, and then walked in the hospital corridor.

Her progress amazed the doctors, but they were certain she would never bowl again. Regardless, she was determined to try.

I never met Kay Vandiver, though we grew up in the same part of the country. All I have of her story is my recollection of what I read in the newspaper – the *Minot (N.D.) Daily News* – about how a local woman with great determination fought valiantly to come back from her terrible accident.

But that newspaper account is enough for me to imagine the accident scene, the red lights of the ambulance and those of police cars flashing in the night, the rescue workers striving to free the unconscious young woman from the wreckage, her worried parents waiting for her return but receiving instead the late night phone call and the terrible news. I imagine the young woman on the hospital gurney being wheeled away after surgery. I visualize the recovery room. I imagine the young woman lying motionless, breathing lightly, in a coma, her parents taking turns in the chair by her bedside, watching, listening to her breathing, hoping for some sign of her return to consciousness.

I imagine her awakening from the coma after three months. I see her lifting one leg with great concentrated effort, placing her foot with slow deliberation on the cool tiles of the hospital floor, and then the other foot, so that she sits on the edge of the bed with both her feet securely on the floor. Later, with help, she stands, then weeks after that, she takes her first steps, one foot in front of the other. A crutch under her left arm, she struggles back toward the life she once knew.

Then there would be what must have seemed like an eternity of recovery in the hospital – two years punctuated with life-crises and setbacks. Then the long days and weeks and months of physical therapy.

Then, of course, I imagine how badly she must have wanted to return to bowling. Never mind the doctors' telling her she couldn't do it; she was determined to show them she could. She would have to learn to bowl all over again, left-handed. And she did.

She had to analyze the necessary moves, break them down into their manageable small components – the adjustments in footwork, approach and follow through – all of which in her former life were predicated on right-handedness. Surely she had bad days and low scores along the way.

But five years to the day after the accident, in the summer of 1966, she entered the North Dakota Women's State Tournament. Last game, last frame of the evening she threw a strike. Her winning score was 295, and she was crowned the Women's Bowling Champion of North Dakota.

When I tell this story to my audiences, I use it as a prime example of the power of determination and perseverance in overcoming handicaps. It is one of the best stories I know that proves the indomitability of the human spirit.

*   *   *

Bill W.: Co-founder of Alcoholics Anonymous

Drinking alcoholic beverages temporarily solved many of Bill W.'s problems. It calmed his nerves, dulled his anger, and replaced his fear with false confidence.

However, his excessive drinking eventually caught up with him. He began suffering more consequences than the drink was worth. But he couldn't stop – no matter how hard he tried, no matter how determined he was to quit.

The mental obsession that comes with alcoholism was torturous to Bill. He describes it well in *Alcoholics Anonymous*, sometimes called "The Big Book":

> I woke up. This had to be stopped. I saw I could not take so much as one drink. I was through forever. Before then, I had written lots of sweet promises, but this time... I meant business. And so I did.
>
> Shortly afterward I came home drunk. There had been no fight. Where had been my high resolve? I simply didn't know. It hadn't even come to mind. Someone had pushed a drink my way, and I had taken it.
>
> Was I crazy? I began to wonder, for such an appalling lack of perspective seemed near being just that.

Bill was not a weak or incapable man. In fact, before his drinking sent him in a downward spiral, he was a successful stock broker. Even after this willful effort to quit, and the remorse that came after he failed, he continued drinking for another two years.

Despite stealing from his wife's purse, blowing business opportunities, ruining personal relationships and his health, once Bill took one drink, he couldn't stop even in light of the consequences that were sure to follow.

Like many alcoholics, for a long time Bill didn't understand the nature of alcoholism nor how to deal with it – except to try to stop drinking. Early on, he surely didn't grasp that the problem was not only an addiction but a physical, psychological and spiritual malady.

He would later describe some of the manifestations of alcoholism in "The Big Book":

> We were having trouble with personal relationships, we couldn't control our emotional natures, we were a prey to misery and depression, we couldn't make a living, we had a feeling of uselessness, we were full of fear, we were unhappy, we couldn't seem to be of real help to other people.

Bill's life changed drastically one November evening in 1934. He received a phone call from Ebby T., a friend with whom he had attended school. He wanted to visit Bill, and so they had dinner at Bill's house that night. Bill was surprised to learn that Ebby was sober, and he was even more amazed with

Ebby's appearance:

"[He was] fresh-skinned and glowing. There was something about his eyes. He was inexplicably different."

Ebby explained that he was attending meetings of the Oxford Group, which encouraged "a simple religious idea and a practical program of action." Although Bill wasn't particularly fond of ministers or formal religion, he had always believed in a power greater than himself.

Ebby asked Bill a pivotal question that would change his life and ultimately the lives of many, many more:

"Why don't you choose your own conception of God?"

This suggestion allowed Bill to move beyond the limited concept of God he had learned as a youth – and to begin to develop a personal relationship with God.

Shortly after his talk with Ebby, Bill entered a hospital to be treated for alcoholic withdrawals. While beginning to practice the tenets of the Oxford Group, Bill had another thought that would eventually change the lives of many.

"While I lay in the hospital, the thought came that there were thousands of hopeless alcoholics who might be glad to have what had been so freely given me. Perhaps I could help some of them. They, in turn, might work with others," Bill said.

In June of 1935 Bill drove to Akron, Ohio, to close a business deal. The deal did not go through, and Bill found himself in danger of drinking. Keeping to his conviction, he sought out another alcoholic for mutual support. He stumbled upon Dr. Bob, an Akron physician, who had tried to quit drinking many times prior to meeting Bill. After spending time with Bill, Dr. Bob never drank again. These two men are credited with being the co-founders of Alcoholics Anonymous. They spent the summer scouting the Akron City Hospital for alcoholics and continued to share their experiences, wisdom and understanding. As a result, the first A.A. group was formed. Over the next couple years, other groups were formed in New York, Cleveland and elsewhere.

As A.A. gained momentum, Bill believed it was necessary to publish a book chronicling the experiences of numerous alcoholics and outlining a program of action. Many people contributed to the book. Bill consulted priests, medical doctors, psychologists, and A.A.'s first 100 members. The spiritual program of action was similar to the Oxford Group's. Bill was convinced of "the need for moral inventory, confession of personality defects, restitution to those harmed, helpfulness to others, and the necessity of belief in and dependence upon God."

Although Bill was at first hesitant to pursue a personal relationship with God, it became the focus of the book, *Alcoholics Anonymous*. Bill was certain that he had not overcome his handicap on his own power. Bill had lived on his own power until late 1934 – and failed miserably in his quest for sobriety, success and peace of mind. When he finally became open to developing a relationship with a power greater than himself – and began practicing a spiritual program of action – his results were much different.

After publication of the book, A.A.'s growth exploded. By 2001, there were approximately two million members and more than 100,000 groups in 150 countries.

Reflecting on that fateful day in November of 1934 when Ebby reached out to Bill to share a common solution to their common problem, Bill wrote:

"Each day my friend's simple talk in our kitchen multiplies itself in a widening circle of peace on earth and good will to men."

Bill W. died in 1971 after 37 years of sobriety.

His story illustrates the conquest of two of life's hurdles: first, the handicap of alcoholism; and, second, the hurdle of lack of self-knowledge – particularly as it relates to knowing who we are in relation to a power greater than ourselves.

*　　*　　*

Oprah Winfrey: How she overcame a terrible childhood

Some years ago I was flipping through the TV channels when I came upon the *Oprah* show. This particular episode featured a panel of people who had been sexually abused by their own relatives.

They took turns telling their sordid stories about what had happened to them. Then it was Oprah's turn. She revealed her own story of having been sexually abused as a child – much to the surprise of many, including me.

What she said was shocking – and perplexing at the same time. What I didn't understand was how in the world could a person coming out of such a terrible background turn out to be one of the most successful, most powerful women in the world. How did she make the transition from where she was – seemingly without hope – to where she is today? How did she manage to break the stranglehold that her depressing past must have had on her?

I just had to know, so I did some research.

Born in rural Mississippi and reared by her grand-mother until she was six years old, Oprah began her life with all the promise of a happy existence. Though impoverished and teased by her peers for her ragged clothing, Oprah possessed a natural zest for life and fell in love with play acting and reciting poetry and

Biblical passages to a local church audience. Her grandmother taught her to read, and at two years old she could read aloud to her Sunday listeners.

At the age of six, however, Oprah's mother, Vernita, sent for her, so Oprah moved to Milwaukee, where she lived in a poor and dangerous neighborhood. With her mom absent all day working, Oprah was left alone at home, where, from ages 9 to 13, she was sexually abused by male relatives and one of her mother's so-called friends.

By age 14, Oprah had had enough, so she ran away from home. She got pregnant not long after this, then went to live with her father in Nashville. Oprah kept her pregnancy a secret as long as she could. She gave birth to a son prematurely, and he died shortly thereafter due to complications caused by the premature birth.

While the loss of her baby was traumatic, her life finally took a turn for the better while living with her father.

Because of his insistence that Oprah perform well academically, Vernon Winfrey became the catalyst by which Oprah started a new life. He implemented a strict curfew and required Oprah to read a book each week and compose a book report to demonstrate her understanding of the material.

In this new environment, under her father's tutelage, Oprah blossomed. She excelled in school, taking honors classes and joining the drama and debate clubs as well as the student council. Her real love and talent lay with the performing arts and public speaking. Her outstanding oratory skills as displayed in the Elks Club speaking contest earned her a full scholarship to Tennessee State University.

She graduated in 1976 and went to work in Baltimore as co-host of a TV talk show. Her viewing audience grew substantially because of her animated and lively way of speaking and her warm, compassionate nature. In 1984, she left the security and stability of the job in Baltimore to take a chance on a floundering TV talk show in Chicago known as *AM Chicago*.

Oprah embraced her role as host of the 30-minute show and soon became a favorite of Chicago's early risers. Within a year *AM Chicago* was an hour long and was now called *The Oprah Winfrey Show*.

The rest of her phenomenal success is history: performing the moving role of Sofia in *The Color Purple*, producing the movie titled *Their Eyes Were Watching God*, and forming her own production company, Harpo Productions, Inc.

And as her fame and fortune grew, so did her generosity. She started Oprah's Angel Network, a program that has given tens of millions of dollars to various philanthropic causes. These include building a school for South African girls and providing financial assistance to Gulf Coast families devastated by Hurricane Katrina. In addition, she has used her considerable energy and influence to successfully promote legislation to protect children from the kind of abuse she suffered as a child.

Looking back over the panorama of Oprah's life, we see that she overcame major obstacles through determination and, as she says, "by the grace of God." Her triumph over adversity and abuse should give us all hope that we can get over the hurdles of life – no matter how insurmountable they may seem.

Chapter 8

The Fourth Hurdle:
Lack of Self-knowledge

he most difficult of life's four hurdles may be the lack of self-knowledge – the state of not knowing who we are and not recognizing our strengths and limitations.

Without the compass of self-knowledge, we are adrift in a flood of busyness and blind ambition, our direction uncertain, our destination unknown. We incessantly pursue wealth and fame, the mere trappings of success.

We are easily distracted by praise and admiration, though they can neither add to nor diminish our value as human beings. We tend to forget that real self-confidence derives not from the opinions of others but from knowledge of our true selves.

Self-knowledge requires putting in the time to

think, to reflect, to mull over the big questions of life. And this requires solitude, time spent away from the madding crowd, away from the hustle and bustle of life.

Among those who understand the value of quiet reflection is Clayton Christensen, a professor in the Harvard Business School. While studying at Oxford, despite a heavy course load, he took time out of every day to ponder his destiny and deepen his self-knowledge.

"I decided to spend an hour every night reading, thinking and praying about why God put me on this Earth.... I stuck with it and ultimately figured out the purpose of my life," he wrote in the *Harvard Business Review.* "My purpose grew out of my religious faith, but faith isn't the only thing that gives people direction."

It's true that a key component of self-knowledge is to know who we are in relation to our Creator. Who are we? Where did we come from? Are we just another animal species, albeit an intelligent one, on this planet, or do we possess a spark of the divine?

Henry David Thoreau, the American philosopher and poet, pondered these questions for years. And in a moment of pristine inspiration, he wrote this eloquent statement of wisdom and faith:

> *I know that I am. I know that another is who knows more than I, who takes an interest in me, whose creature, and yet whose kindred in one sense, am I.*

Another great American writer and thinker, Og Mandino, in his bestselling book, *The Greatest Salesman In The World*, deals with the subject of self-knowledge. The storyline in the book features a salesman who aspires to be the best in his field. He discovers the secret scrolls of wisdom that will guide him to great success. One of the scrolls speaks to the uniqueness and inherent nobility of humankind and the subject of human destiny.

> *I am nature's greatest miracle.*
> *Although I am of the animal kingdom, animal rewards alone will not satisfy me....*
> *I am a unique creature of nature.*
> *I am rare, and there is value in all rarity; therefore, I am valuable. I am the end product of thousands of years of evolution; therefore, I am better equipped in both mind and body than all the emperors and wise men who preceded me....*
> *I am not on this earth by chance. I am here for a purpose, and that purpose is to grow into a mountain, not to shrink to a grain of sand....*

If the hurdle of lack of self-knowledge is challenging for most of us, it is especially so for celebrities. When they're on top, celebrities are awash in praise and admiration. Everybody, it seems, loves a winner.

The two celebrities – Mariah Carey and Pete Maravich – whose stories are told below were both winners, in the common understanding of the term. They were performers whose performances transcended what was formerly imagined possible, bringing them great fame and wealth. Both received high praise and acclaim.

But both learned that fame and fortune were insufficient to bring them the true success and peace of mind that come with self-knowledge. Their stories demonstrate a common truth: We must know ourselves in order to be truly successful and happy.

*   *   *

Mariah Carey: There's such a thing as too busy

When Mariah Carey was 30, she was regarded as the most popular female vocalist of the 1990s. By 2002, her albums had sold more than any recording artist ever except the Beatles and Elvis Presley.

Mariah's beginnings were humble and obscure. Biracial – her father was black, her mother white – she was born in 1970 on Long Island, New York. Her parents divorced when she was three. Her father was Alfred Roy Carey, a Venezuelan aeronautical engineer who grew up mostly in Harlem; her mother, Patricia Carey, an Irish American voice coach and opera singer from the Midwest. She was reared mainly by her mother, who worked multiple jobs to pay the rent. At two, she had begun imitating her mother's operatic singing; at four, her mother was giving her singing lessons.

During high school Mariah wrote songs and dreamed of being a professional singer. After high school she continued writing and dreaming, but worked as a waitress and coat check girl to earn money. She also studied cosmetology, just in case her dream of being a singer didn't materialize.

She explained years later that one reason she pushed herself as hard as she did, trying to be somebody, was that she never felt special. Only her music made her feel special.

"I didn't feel pretty. I didn't feel like I fit in with other kids, because I really didn't. We didn't have a lot of money growing up at all. Sometimes I had to live with different friends of my mother... when we didn't have a place to stay," she explained in an interview on *Larry King Live* in 2002.

Music was her essential thing, her ticket. When she was 18 she started singing backup to Brenda Starr. Brenda became her friend and mentor, and it was through Brenda that she got her career-launching break. Mariah had a demo tape of her singing, and Brenda was determined to see that the tape got into the hands of someone who could help Mariah.

So, the two of them went to a party thrown by WTG Records in New York. Brenda introduced Mariah to one of the principals of the company and handed him the demo tape. The tape was passed on to another principal of the company, Tommy Motolla, who listened to it that night. He was very impressed and shortly thereafter signed her up to work on her first album.

The album, *Mariah Carey* (1990), was a hit, and she became a celebrity almost overnight. In 1993, she married Tommy Motolla.

Mariah achieved extraordinary fame and wealth, as measured by the charts, but these had not brought her true success and happiness, certainly not peace of mind.

By 1998, Mariah had divorced her husband (also her first agent) and left his record company. With all her previous success, she had no trouble finding a new record label.

But she soon found that with her new record company came a lot more work and a lot less rest. She felt the absence of a personal assistant who could intervene for her and call a timeout when she needed a break. She struggled greatly with her workload because she found it impossible to turn down anything she thought would advance her career.

"It's hard to say no. I thought if I said no everything would crumble around me," she said.

She allowed herself to be controlled. Under the stresses and strains of overcommitment, she collapsed at her mother's house, and she was checked into a hospital to rest and recuperate. She later described the collapse as "both emotional and physical."

She explained later why she decided to go to the hospital and stay awhile.

"I said, 'You know, maybe if I go, people will understand that I am a human being, and I need a break.'"

While recovering, Mariah realized that she had been trying to do more than she was capable of – and more than should be asked of her. Her collapse thus brought self-knowledge – of her limitations and of who she was.

Rather than allowing others to control her, she finally learned to say no, took control of her life, and recognized the truth about herself, about her human limitations.

Mariah never doubted she'd bounce back.

"I have so much faith. And I'll never lose my faith.... I know it's not like the cool thing to be a person like that. But I'm a believer, I believe in God, and that's how I get through things. But that's the truth with me," she said on *Larry King Live* in 2009.

So, the lesson here is to be honest with yourself about yourself, because this is one of the foundations upon which true success and happiness depend.

If we allow ourselves to be identified too closely with worldly fame and wealth, if these are the criteria against which we measure ourselves, we lose our essential selves and become vulnerable to despair and self-doubt. Without self-knowledge we may acquire the outward signs of success but miss the deep happiness that comes with true success.

*   *   *

'Pistol Pete' Maravich: Basketball superstar

Pete Maravich accomplished things on the basketball court that nobody, except maybe his father, Coach Press Maravich, thought were possible.

A unique and original athlete, Pete transcended the game. He was not merely a player, but a performer as well. The results of his performances on the court were fame and fortune. He loved the adulation; he worked at wowing the crowds. But, at the end of the day, the fame and wealth he achieved were insufficient definitions of who he was. Fame and wealth – the conventional accoutrements of a certain kind of success – failed to bring the happiness and peace of mind that mark true success.

For this, he needed to overcome the fourth hurdle of life: lack of self-knowledge. And to gain true self-knowledge he would eventually have to turn to a higher power. Without connection to this higher power, this superior being, self-knowledge would be incomplete. Indeed, as Maravich would discover, fame and wealth can actually obscure self-knowledge.

*   *   *

Coach Press Maravich believed his son had inherited "the basketball gene." Press himself had been an outstanding player, and he became a visionary and innovative coach. But it took Pete's desire and talent to realize his father's vision and to transcend the game.

"You would not suspect he could do the things he did – until he did them," wrote newspaper columnist Jerry McLeese. It was McLeese, a writer for the Anderson (S.C.) *Independent*, who first put the nickname "Pistol Pete" in print. He observed that Maravich – a starter as an eighth-grader, listed on the Daniel High varsity team roster at 5'6" and 103 pounds – still shot the ball two-handed from his hip, like a gunslinger.

"He was doing stuff you had never seen before, things that mesmerized you," like the behind-the-back pass, McLeese wrote. "Other players would have to literally stop because they were so amazed. He turned players into spectators."

Later Maravich would recall a spectacular moment from his freshman year in high school:

"I threw a behind-the-back bounce pass on the move through a guy's legs!... I was coming down on a three-on-one break, and my man was overplaying me to the left and giving me the open teammate on the right.... As my man was sliding and I was dribbling, I noticed his legs moving in and out, in and out. Still on the move, I saw the right moment and threw the ball when his legs were out – behind my back, now, not a straight pass – and I put it right through him to a teammate on the left. He converted for the basket. The crowd, boy... The crowd, I want to tell you, they went berserk. I couldn't believe it. My man looked like somebody stepped on his head."

*   *   *

At LSU Maravich set an all-time NCAA career scoring record with 3,667 points, an average of 44.2 points a game for 83 games. To get an idea about the magnitude of that, imagine that you have a son or a grandson going to college who aspires to beat Pete's record. All he'd have to do is make fifteen 3-pointers in each game for four years. (Actually, someone figured that had the 3-point shot been in play in his day, Pete's average might have been around 52 points a game.)

Maravich may have been the greatest basketball player who ever lived. Biographer Mark Kriegel lists some of the highlights of Pete's college career: He was ranked first, fourth and fifth for the most points in a single season in NCAA history; on February 7, 1970, he scored 69 points against Alabama; he was a unanimous first team All-American in 1968, 1969 and 1970, the year he led LSU to the National Invitational Tournament's Final Four, LSU's first postseason appearance in 16 years; and he won the

Naismith Award in 1970.

"Pistol Pete" was regarded by many as the game's greatest ball-handler, and people came just to see him play. When he was in the game it was "Showtime." The crowds exceeded the capacities of the venues in which he played – from the LSU "Cow Palace" to Pauley Pavilion.

Press Maravich, coach at LSU during Pete's years there, became obsessed with Pete's numbers on offense.

"In Pete's first season of varsity ball, LSU improved from 3-23 to 14-12, while violating the game's every orthodoxy," wrote biographer Kriegel.

Though Pete kept scoring and setting records, he became disheartened. His high offensive production and showmanship came with a cost. Tension developed between father and son. An additional cost of his fame was that Pete couldn't go anywhere without being recognized. One of the assistant coaches, Rusty Bergman, observed:

"The pressure just kept building. It got to the point where Pete was like Elvis. He had to move out of the jock dorm his senior year just to get some peace and quiet."

Meanwhile, Pete's mother, Helen, was discovered to be drinking heavily.

"Confronted, Helen finally lashed out. She was another human sacrifice to The Game. This obsession shared by her husband and her son had shut her out and shut her down," wrote biographer Kriegel.

For years, Helen had harbored a fear of abandonment, beginning when she was nine years old. Her mother, abandoned by her father, was unable to take care of her. *De facto* an orphan, she was reared by an aunt in western Pennsylvania. Tragically, the stress of the family dynamic would eventually drive Helen to take her own life. In the autumn of 1974, in Pete's fourth and last season with the Atlanta Hawks, Helen shot herself in the head with a .22-caliber pistol.

"Press was totally, mentally blown away. I didn't realize how much he loved her until he had lost her. He was like a zombie," Coach Bergman pointed out.

*   *   *

The value of the contract that Pete Maravich signed to play for the Atlanta Hawks was reported to be $1.9 million. At the time, it was the richest in sports history.

The expectations of fans and the resentment of his teammates – whose salaries were a fraction of what Maravich was being paid – placed enormous pressure on the rookie. In his pro debut against the Milwaukee Bucks and Lew Alcindor, Pete scored just seven points as the Hawks lost 107-98.

"Pete castigated himself in the postgame media gathering. The world had been hoping for an exhibition from Press's boy. Instead, closer inspection would have revealed a confused creature with Helen's haunted eyes," biographer Kriegel wrote. "Pete said, 'I felt like a ghost was sitting on me.'"

Pete played in the professional leagues 10 seasons before retiring in 1980. In 1970-71 he was All-Rookie; he was All-NBA first team twice and second team twice; in the 1972-73 season and the 1974-75 season he ranked seventh in assists; in 1976-77 he ranked first in scoring, with a 31.1 per game average; his career scoring average per game was 24.2, which placed him seventeenth on the career list.

But he never played on a championship team, and he was haunted throughout his career by a sense of failure to live up to his expectations and the expectations of others.

*   *   *

When I coached the LSU Tigers basketball team, I asked Pete to come and speak to the players before an important ball game. I had replaced his father as head coach at LSU – which had always given me an uneasy feeling. I never liked the idea of taking someone else's job after he'd been fired.

I really had no idea what Pete would say. But I hoped the game's greatest offensive player would motivate the team with something positive, inspire them to their best effort. What he said helped me get to a deeper understanding of the most difficult of the four hurdles of life – lack of self-knowledge.

Pete stood up and faced the team.

"I was on the cover of *Sports Illustrated* several times," he began.

Rapid-fire, he ticked off his string of accomplishments: the biggest pro contract in NBA history, led the nation in scoring, been All-American, received the Naismith Award, made All-NBA, was a multimillionaire, drove a Porsche, walked around with three or four thousand dollars in his pocket, drank, chased women, lived in mansions in Atlanta and New Orleans and in a luxurious apartment in Boston.

He paused, then lowered his voice.

"But, guys, I was a miserable human being. I thought I had it all. I had everything. I thought it was all about dipping my toes in a pool while some thinly clad woman hands me a mint julep. What more could I wish for? But I wasn't happy."

The accumulation of material wealth, the bucketsful of acclaim and praise, the standing crowds cheering for him, the money, the self-indulgences of the rich – all of these combined didn't bring him happiness or peace of mind.

He went on, talking more slowly now, as if to contrast his newborn peace of mind with his former stressful and frenetic existence.

"I was miserable, until one night, in Metairie, Louisiana, I was so fed up with life, I said aloud to myself, 'This can't be Pistol Pete Maravich. He had everything society tells us is success.'"

He had attained wealth, fame and status. But it

wasn't good fortune, happiness and kindness, as the old *Webster's* dictionary had defined success.

He decided he would commit suicide.

"Four o'clock in the morning," he said, "sitting on the bed in one of the rooms in our house, I was just going to put the pistol in my mouth. I was so down in the dumps. For some reason I set the pistol down on the bed. I didn't know how to pray. I didn't even know if there was a God. But I fell on the bed, prone, face down. And I said, 'God, if there is a God, I don't even know if you're there. I've spit at you, laughed at you, mocked you. But, God, if you're there, would you somehow, in some way, please touch my life.

"Instantly – I don't know how to express it – the sun didn't dance in the sky, the sea didn't part. But a peace took over my body, for the first time in my life. Before that moment, I had been a miserable S.O.B., until I took God into my life four years ago. Guys, whatever you do, do not let your possessions possess you, or you'll end up miserable, as I did."

That was it, his bottom line. He thanked them for their attention, wished them well, and walked out of the room.

The logic of his message was clear: You are not defined by your earthly possessions and achievements nor by the praise or blame or adulation of others. You are not who others say you are, or should be. Rather, you are who God made you to be, and therefore you cannot know who you are without accepting your

Creator into your life.

During the last four years of his life, I got to know Pete as a friend. After his epiphany he was a wonderful person to be around; he wanted above all else to help others avoid the mistakes he had made. He was an evangelist in the best sense of the word. Pete was the real thing – a deep believer. And he lived his beliefs. He had about him a true sense of spirituality.

I asked Pete to speak to the team because I felt he would be an inspiring speaker. He fervently wanted to motivate others to choose to accept God into their lives, as he had. He felt, as I do, that self-knowledge can never be complete without some understanding of the role of the God who created us.

So, Pete's message – which I concur with wholeheartedly – is, finally, about choice. We can have success and happiness if we choose them.

Epilogue

Choosing the right road

n the pages of this book, I have tried to describe the most common obstacles to success and happiness, the hurdles, and to illustrate how others have gotten over them. But I want to emphasize that as surely as life presents us with hurdles it also provides us with choices, or various approaches to solving our problems.

We can choose true success and happiness or we can choose a life that is something less than fulfilling. It really is up to us.

Here's what I mean: As we go down the road of life, we come to a three-pronged fork in the road. The one to the right is called *If it feels good, do it.* It's the road of instant gratification, the easy way out. Every time I've taken a step down this path I've ended up frustrated, disillusioned and bewildered. I strongly recommend not going this way.

The road to the left is called *Despair*, giving up. Its mantra is purely negative, fear-based and self-pitying: "I'm bankrupt, my wife left me, my boyfriend dumped me, I can't stop drinking, I feel so empty, I must be no good." This is the road that takes us away from a positive vision of life. It is a road to be avoided at all cost.

The road in the middle – the straight and narrow – is the highly recommended route. It's called *I can be successful. I deserve to be successful. I can have peace, health and prosperity. I can be fortunate, happy and kind.* This is the path to true success and happiness.

Of course, it takes commitment, perseverance and faith to successfully navigate this road. But the payoff makes it worth the effort.

The truth is, we can choose our own path in life. In other words, our future is in our own hands – in all but the most extreme of cases. The very thought of this lifts my spirits every time I think of it.

The philosopher Henry David Thoreau expressed this same thought with such clarity:

> *I know of no more encouraging fact than the unquestionable ability of man to elevate his life by a conscious endeavor.*

*   *   *

In closing, I'd like to expand a bit on what I described earlier as perhaps the most difficult of the hurdles of life: lack of self-knowledge. I am convinced that to be truly happy it is necessary to know not only who we are in relation to our fellowman and the world around us, but who we are in relation to the God who created us. To arrive at this knowledge independently, we must ask ourselves a few very important questions: From where and from whom did we come? Where and to whom will we return when our time on this Earth is over?

The answers to these questions, as stated earlier in this book, were suggested by Mr. Thoreau. While thought of more as a philosopher than a theologian, he proclaimed a profound truth that should be comforting to us all: While we are God's creatures, we are also his kindred, his children.

And, of course, it is the nature of children to be dependent on their parents, and the nature of parents to love and be there for their children.

One of my favorite authors – considered to be one of the twentieth century's most influential New Thought writers – is Emmet Fox (1886-1951). His lectures each Sunday morning during the Great Depression – at such venues as the Manhattan Opera House and Carnegie Hall – drew more than 5,000 people each time he spoke, all of them seeking relief from confusion and despair. People lined up for blocks to hear him. He was loaded with wisdom.

His message was that life is consciousness, and we, therefore, are what we think. He said:

> *If you really believe that God is working through you, the quality of your life will be so high, and you will receive so much inspiration through Him, that every barrier in your path will fall away. Undreamed-of good will come into your life, and you will be a blessing to all around you.*

My dear friend and mentor of 40 years, Coach John Wooden, once expressed to me his unshakable belief in a power greater than himself. He advised:

> *There is only one kind of life that truly wins, and that is the one that places faith in the hands of God. Until that is done, we are on an aimless course that runs in circles and goes nowhere.*

I agree with Coach Wooden. My own experience bears this out: Intuition, imagination, perseverance and faith, taken together, are the rock upon which we can build a positive vision of life. And I believe such a vision is a prerequisite to a life of success and happiness.

– THE END –

SOURCES

Books, magazine articles, and other printed documents

Anonymous authors. *Alcoholics Anonymous: The Story of How Many Thousands of Men and Women Have Recovered from Alcoholism*. Third Edition. New York: Alcoholics Anonymous World Services, Inc., 1976.

Barrier, Michael. *The Animated Man: A Life of Walt Disney*. Berkeley: University of California, 2007.

Christensen, Clayton M. "How Will You Measure Your Life?" *Harvard Business Review*, July/August 2010.

Donald, David Herbert. *Lincoln*. New York: Simon & Schuster, 1995.

Ehrenreich, Barbara. *Nickel and Dimed: On (Not) Getting By in America*. New York: Henry Holt, 2002.

Gabler, Neal. *Walt Disney*. New York: Alfred A. Knopf, 2006.

Guralnick, Peter. *Last Train to Memphis: The Rise of Elvis Presley*. Boston: Little, Brown and Co., 1994.

Isaacson, Walter. *Einstein, His Life and Universe*. New York: Simon & Schuster, 2007.

Kriegel, Mark. *Pistol: The Life of Pete Maravich*. New York: Free Press, 2007.

Manchester, William. *American Caesar: Douglas MacArthur 1880-1964*. Boston: Little, Brown and Co., 1968.

Mandino, Og. *The Greatest Salesman in the World*. New York: Frederick Fell, Inc., 1968.

Milton, John. *John Milton: Complete Poems and Major Prose.* Editor Merritt Y. Hughes. New York: Odyssey, 1957.

"No Deterrent." (Caption under photo of Kay Vandiver's return to bowling, left-handed.) *Niagra Falls Gazette.* August 28, 1966, page 6-E.

O'Neal, Shaquille. *Shaq Talks Back.* New York: St. Martin's Press, 2001.

Peale, Norman Vincent. *The Power of Positive Thinking* (Condensed Gift Edition). Norwalk, Conn.: The C.R. Gibson Company, 1952.

Plato. *Republic.* Translated by Paul Shorey. *Plato: The Collected Dialogues.* Edited by Edith Hamilton and Huntington Cairns. Princeton: Princeton University Press, 1996.

Rousseau, Jean-Jacques. *A Discourse on Inequality.* Translated by Maurice Cranston. Harmondsworth, Middlesex, England: Penguin Books, 1984.

Sandel, Michael. *Justice: What's the Right Thing to Do?* New York: Farrar, Straus, and Giroux, 2010.

Sypher, Wylie. *Loss of the Self in Modern Literature and Art.* New York, Vintage, 1964.

Thoreau, Henry David. *Thoreau: On Man & Nature.* Mount Vernon, New York: Peter Pauper Press, 1960.

Vonnegut, Kurt. *Mother Night.* New York: Dell, 1974.

Online articles, speeches and interviews

Brown, Gaylen. "Minot History Through Slides, 1900-1920." (Script which accompanies the Minot History Slide Show), 1983.

Carey, Mariah. Interview: Parts 1 and 2. *Larry King Live.* December 19, 2002. CNN.com Transcripts.

"Don Meyer, Winner of Jimmy V Award 2009." Youtube.com. August 12, 2009.

"Elvis Presley Told to Stick to Truck Driving." Snopes.com.

Horner, Matina S., and Belinda Friedrich. *Oprah Winfrey (Women of Achievement)*. Chelsea House Publications, 2001. *EBSCOhost*. Web. August 2011. www.ebscohost.com.

Olney, Buster. "Twelve wins away: Don Meyer's hard road back from the brink." *ESPN The Magazine*.

"Paul Anderson (1932-1994)." *The New Georgia Encyclopedia*. November 18, 2002.

Rowling, J. K. Harvard Commencement Address, June 5, 2008. "The Fringe Benefits of Failure, and the Importance of Imagination." *Harvard Magazine*. May 27, 2010.

---,Interview. *Larry King Live*. October 20, 2000. CNN.com Transcripts.

Ruettiger, Rudy. Personal interviews by Trent Angers, editor. June & August, 2011.

"Steven Speilberg to Graduate from California State University, Long Beach, With Bachelor's Degree in Film and Electronic Arts." *CSU Newsline*. May 14, 2002.

REFERENCES

Chapter 2. In search of a positive vision of life

p. 37 – "...*lift you to victory.*": Dr. Norman Vincent Peale, *The Power of Positive Thinking*, Norwalk, Conn.: The C.R. Gibson Co., 1952, page 4. (I first met Dr. Peale at an event on the LSU campus in the late 1980s; his writings were a big influence on my life before and after that first meeting.)

Chapter 4. The 4 Hurdles of Life

pp. 51-56 – *Don Meyer story*: Video of the 2009 V Foundation Award presentation (named for the late Jimmy Valvano, a.k.a. "Jimmy V," who was head coach of the North Carolina basketball team and who later died of cancer.)

Chapter 5. The First Hurdle: 'I can't / You can't'

pp. 60-62 – *Elvis Presley story*: Peter Guralnick. *Last Train to Memphis: The Rise of Elvis Presley*. Boston: Little, Brown and Co., 1994.

pp. 62-65 – *Albert Einstein story*: Walter Isaacson, *Einstein, His Life and Universe*. New York: Simon & Schuster, 2007.

pp. 65-68 – *Walt Disney story*: Neal Gabler, *Walt Disney*. New York: Alfred A. Knopf, 2006.

pp. 69-75 – *Rudy Ruettiger story*: Interviews by Trent Angers, editor. June and August 2011.

Chapter 6. The Second Hurdle: Past Failures / Fear of Failure

pp. 80-84 – *J.K. Rowling story*: From her Harvard commencement address, June 5, 2008, titled "The Fringe Benefits of Failure, and the Importance of Imagination." (The part of her talk dealing with failure is written about here, while the segment on imagination is omitted, only because it is not germane to this chapter; the latter, however, makes for fascinating reading and is a brilliant personal discourse on the function of imagination.)

Also, *Larry King Live* interview, October 20, 2000. CNN.com Transcripts.

pp. 85-86 – *Steven Spielberg story*: "Steven Spielberg to Graduate from California State University, Long Beach, with Bachelor's Degree in Film and Electronic Arts." *CSU Newsletter*. May 14, 2002.

Chapter 7. The Third Hurdle: Handicaps

pp. 90-96 and 105-106 – *Paul Anderson story*: "Paul Anderson (1932-1994)." *The New Georgia Encyclopedia*, November 18, 2002.

pp. 106-109 – *Kay Vandiver story*: Minot (N.D.) *Daily News*, August 1966 (exact date and title unknown).

Also, "No Deterrent." *Niagra Falls (N.Y.) Gazette*, August 28, 1966, page 6-E.

pp. 110-114 – *Bill W. story*: Alcoholics Anonymous (Third Edition). New York: Alcoholics Anonymous World Services, Inc., 1976.

pp. 115-118 – *Oprah Winfrey story*: Matina S. Horner and Belinda Friedrich. *Oprah Winfrey (Women of Achievement)*. Chelsea House Publications, 2001. *EBSCOhost*. Web. August 2011. www.ebscohost.com

Chapter 8. The Fourth Hurdle:
Lack of Self-Knowledge

p. 120 – *"...faith isn't the only thing that gives people direction."*: Clayton M. Christensen. "How Will You Measure Your Life?" *Harvard Business Review*, July/August 2010.

p. 120 – *"...whose kindred in one sense, am I."*: Henry David Thoreau. *Thoreau: On Man & Nature*. Mount Vernon, New York: Peter Pauper Press, 1960, page 61.

p. 121 – *"...not to shrink to a grain of sand...."*: Og Mandino. *The Greatest Salesman in the World*. New York: Frederick Fell, Inc., 1968, pages 71-73.

pp. 122-126 – *Mariah Carey story*: Mariah Carey. Interviews on *Larry King Live*, December 19, 2002.

pp. 126-134 – *"Pistol Pete" Maravich story*: Mark Kriegel. *Pistol: The Life of Pete Maravich*. New York: Free Press, 2007.

p. 127 – *"He turned players into spectators."*: Jerry McLeese, columnist for the Anderson, S.C., *Independent*.

p. 128 – *"...like somebody stepped on his head."*: Mark Kriegel. *Pistol: The Life of Pete Maravich*. New York: Free Press, 2007.

p. 128 – *"...around 52 points per game."*: Sam King, former sports editor/columnist for the Baton Rouge *State-Times* and *Morning Advocate*, calculated this number based on play-by-play statistics kept courtside by LSU's record-keepers.

pp. 131-133 – *Pete Maravich's pre-game address to the LSU Tigers basketball team*: This account is based primarily on my recollection of what Pete said that night and on one of his talks following the religious experience that turned his life around.

Epilogue. Choosing the right road

p. 136 – *"...by a conscious endeavor."*: Henry David Thoreau. *Thoreau: On Man & Nature*. Mount Vernon, New York: Peter Pauper Press, 1960, page 12.

p. 138 – *"...a blessing to all around you."*: Emmet Fox. Emmet Fox Home Page.

Index

Note: Page numbers in *italics* indicate photographs.

About the Author

COACH DALE BROWN, who served as head coach of the LSU basketball team for 25 years, (1972-1997), is one of the top motivational speakers in the U.S. The creator of a syndicated radio program called Motivational Moments that ran on NPR, he also served for a while as a college basketball analyst for ESPN and CBS.

As LSU coach, he was twice named National Basketball Coach of the Year, led his team to two Final Fours and four Elite Eights, and emerged as

the second-winningest coach in SEC history. He is also known as the recruiter of Shaquille O'Neal, one of the top basketball players ever at LSU and in the NBA.

Coach Brown lives in Baton Rouge, Louisiana, with his wife, Vonnie.

– Photography by Brad Messina, Baton Rouge, La.

DAN MARIN teaches business ethics and business strategy in the management department at Louisiana State University in Baton Rouge. He started at LSU in 1984 as director of the Masters of Business Administration program.

He holds a BA in English from Oberlin College in Ohio, a PhD in English from the University of Iowa, and an MBA from the University of South Carolina.

He has published fiction, nonfiction, and scholarly articles about business theory and business communication, as well as several corporate histories.

TRENT ANGERS, nominated twice for the Nobel Prize in Literature (2000 and 2001), is a veteran journalist who has authored thousands of published news and feature stories, as well as five books, in a writing and editing career that has spanned four decades.

His better-known books are: *The Forgotten Hero Of My Lai: The Hugh Thompson Story*; *Grand Coteau: The Holy Land of South Louisiana*; and *An Airboat on the Streets of New Orleans*.

He received a BA in journalism from LSU in 1970. From 1975 to 2011 he was editor and publisher of *Acadiana Profile*, "The Magazine of the Cajun Country," based in Lafayette, La. Since 1979, he has been editor and publisher of Acadian House Publishing, a publisher of non-fiction books.

Inspiring Books
from
Acadian House Publishing

Getting Over the 4 Hurdles of Life

A 160-page hardcover book that shows us ways to get past the obstacles, or hurdles, that block our path to success, happiness and peace of mind. Four of the most common hurdles are "I can't / You can't," past failures or fear of failure, handicaps, and lack of self-knowledge. This inspiring book – by one of the top motivational speakers in the U.S. – is brought to life by intriguing stories of various people who overcame life's hurdles. Introduction by former LSU and NBA star Shaquille O'Neal. (Author: Coach Dale Brown. ISBN: 0-925417-72-6. Price: $17.95)

Waiting For Eli
A Father's Journey from Fear to Faith

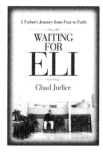

A 176-page hardcover book about a Lafayette, La., couple and their infant son Eli who was born with a dreaded birth defect called spina bifida. It is an inspiring story of faith, hope and the power of prayer. The book takes us on an emotional roller coaster ride, starting with the day the author first learns of his son's medical condition. This moving story has a strong pro-life, pro-love message, and is made even more compelling by the author's descriptions of little miracles along the way. (Author: Chad Judice. ISBN: 0-925417-65-3. Price: $16.95)

Dying In God's Hands

A 152-page hardcover book that provides keen insights into the hearts and minds of the dying. It is based on a dozen or more interviews with terminally ill hospice patients, in which they share their hopes, dreams, fears and needs. The majority of the interviews provide evidence that faith in God and belief in the hereafter are the greatest strengths of the dying. Designed to comfort the dying and their loved ones, the book also contains a section of prayers and prose from all major world religions. (Author: Camille Pavy Claibourne. ISBN: 0-925417-64-5. Price: $16.95)